D0932541

THE
ROYAL FAMILY
ALBUM

BY
HELEN DIGBY

SMITHMARK

Copyright © 1993 Brompton Books Corp.

All rights reserved. No part of this publication may be reproduced, stored in a retrieval system or transmitted in any form by any means, electronic, mechanical, photocopying or otherwise, without first obtaining written permission of the copyright owner.

This edition published in 1993 by SMITHMARK Publishers Inc. 16 East 32nd Street, New York, New York 10016.

SMITHMARK books are available for bulk purchase for sales promotion and premium use. For details write or telephone the Manager of Special Sales, SMITHMARK Publishers Inc., 16 East 32nd Street, New York, NY 10016, (212) 532 6600.

Produced by Brompton Books Corp.,
15 Sherwood Place,
Greenwich, CT 06830

ISBN 0-8317-7484-3

Printed in Hong Kong

10 9 8 7 6 5 4 3 2 1

PAGE 1: *Queen Elizabeth II in Garter robes.*

PAGE 2: *Clockwise, from top left: the royal family gathering to celebrate the Queen Mother's birthday; postcard commemorating the coronation of George V in 1911; the Duke and Duchess of Windsor with other members of the royal family in 1967; the Duke of York with Princess Beatrice; the Princess of Wales in 1991; Queen Victoria, the future Edward VII (right), George V (left) and Edward VIII (foreground); Queen Elizabeth with her grandson, Peter Phillips. Centre: the Queen and Duke of Edinburgh.*

PAGE 3: *Clockwise, from top left: the Queen at the Trooping the Colour ceremony; George V and Queen Mary; the Prince and Princess of Wales; Sem's cartoon of Edward VII; the present Queen with the Duke of Edinburgh, her parents, Queen Elizabeth and George VI, and Princess Margaret, 1947.*

ABOVE: *The Queen and royal family watch a fly-past after her coronation as Elizabeth II in 1953.*

Contents

6 **Introduction**

Chapter One
20 **Edward VII**

Chapter Two
42 **George V**

Chapter Three
70 **Edward VIII**

Chapter Four
98 **George VI**

Chapter Five
124 **The Queen Mother**

Chapter Six
144 **Elizabeth II**

Chapter Seven
190 **Heir Apparent**

Chapter Eight
238 **Royalty Today**

287 Index

288 Acknowledgments

INTRODUCTION

Queen Victoria died on 22 January 1901 after a reign of 63 years, the longest of any British monarch. She breathed her last, surrounded by numerous members of her large family, having survived two sons, one of her daughters, several of her grandchildren, and, of course, her beloved husband Albert. After nearly 40 years in black mourning for her consort, it was ironic that she instructed that black should be excluded as far as possible from her own funeral. As one of her private secretaries remarked, there was nothing the Queen liked better than arranging a funeral, and her own was no exception. She ordered that it should be military and white, with as little pomp as possible. Attended by most of the crowned heads of Europe, she was finally interred next to Albert in the 'dear Mausoleum' at Frogmore on the Windsor Castle estate.

There was a very real sense among contemporaries that an era had come to an end. By the end of the nineteenth century, Queen Victoria had seemed to many of her subjects to be the one permanent fixture in a world of change. *The Times* said that the country had lost a sovereign whom they had almost come to 'worship', as well as a 'personal benefactress'. No-one could quite believe that the formidable old queen was dead, least of all her heir, who had spent nearly 60 years waiting for the job of king.

No-one was entirely sure what to expect from the new king, but in fact Edward VII did little to alter the role of sovereign as established by his mother, who had introduced many traditions which are still upheld today. Victoria and Albert are the foundation stones upon which today's modern monarchy is based. Not only have their direct descendants occupied the British throne throughout this century, but their large family has ensured that there are over 500 descendants – Germans, Danes, Swedes, Spaniards, Russians and Romanians, among others – with some sort of claim to the British throne. Queen Victoria's withdrawal from public life in the aftermath of Albert's death meant that her family had to deputize for her on public and ceremonial occasions, so individual members of the royal family began to enjoy a very much higher public profile than previously. The idea of a royal family (rather than just an individual as monarch) as a force for good and as an example to the nation became very clear during the nineteenth century. Victoria's successors continued this trend and the royal family today acknowledge that, in a sense, their family is also a business, and refer to themselves jokingly as the 'family firm'.

Perhaps more importantly, the conventions of a modern constitutional monarchy were firmly established. The nineteenth century was a turbulent time for sovereigns in Europe. Several thrones were toppled by the waves of republican fervour that periodically swept across the Continent, but the British Crown, although far from exempt from popular criticism, somehow survived. Queen Elizabeth II has apparently joked that she would 'go quietly' if required, but it is unlikely that her great-great-grandmother could have viewed a similar scenario with such equanimity; too many of her relations had been cast out by ungrateful subjects.

The constitutional historian Walter Bagehot advocated a monarchial system of government because he believed that 'Monarchy . . . is an intelligible government . . . the mass of people understand it'. He outlined the three rights of a constitutional monarch: to be consulted, to encourage, and to warn. It is a system that works as long as the principal players, the sovereign and ministers of the Crown, understand their positions. During the nineteenth century the system was still evolving and Queen Victoria's ministers were frequently infuriated by her peremptory memos on every area of policy. Not only

RIGHT: *Queen Victoria – the longest-reigning British monarch.*

did she expect to be consulted, she also expected her suggestions to be heeded and let her displeasure be known when they were not. The fundamental duty of the sovereign, however, is to preserve the institution of monarchy and to understand that the demands of the job should take precedence over personal wishes. The British monarchy has been severely strained once this century: in 1936 Edward VIII refused to bow to the precedents established by his forebears and considered his personal happiness more important than the best interests of the country and the Empire. He carried an almost intolerable burden but, unlike his relations, he found it unacceptable and came close to destroying the very institution which had nurtured him.

The modern monarchy owes its survival to the ability of the kings and queens of this century to move with the times and adapt to the changing circumstances of their day. Socialist governments, the loss of Empire, even the more humdrum question of Establishment attitudes to divorce, have all affected the monarch's rôle. At the same time, there is a strong element of continuity. The Crown is still the fount of all honours, and although most are bestowed on the advice of the government, the most prestigious are in the personal gift of the Queen. The ceremonial of the Crown has changed little in the past 100 years: even at the end of the twentieth century, pomp and pageantry are still an important part of sovereignty.

OPPOSITE PAGE: *Her marriage to Prince Albert in 1840 was a turning point in Victoria's life.*

ABOVE LEFT: *The newly-weds are cheered on their way to Windsor. Protocol demanded that Victoria propose to Albert.*

ABOVE: *Queen Victoria's coronation in 1838. She noted in her diary: 'the Crown being placed on my head . . . was, I must own, a most beautiful, impressive moment'.*

RIGHT: *Of small stature, Victoria nevertheless had a commanding presence and impressed all those who met her.*

THIS PAGE: *Although Victoria was completely devoted to Albert, she was reluctant to let him become involved in affairs of state.*

OPPOSITE: *The youthful Queen Victoria in her coronation robes.*

LEFT: *Victoria and Albert had nine children, whose marriages were to link the British royal family with most of Europe's ruling dynasties.*

OPPOSITE PAGE, BELOW LEFT AND RIGHT: *the Prince Consort's premature death from typhoid in 1861 was a cruel blow; Victoria mourned him for the rest of her life.*

RIGHT: *An official portrait of the Queen, taken to commemorate the Diamond Jubilee.*

BELOW RIGHT: *After Albert's death, Victoria led a life of seclusion, avoiding public duties.*

BELOW: *Victoria and her daughter contemplate a portrait of Vicky's recently deceased husband, Kaiser Frederick of Germany.*

LEFT: *Victoria's affection for her ghillie, John Brown, caused much speculation.*

ABOVE, RIGHT AND FAR RIGHT: *The matriarch of a vast extended family, Victoria was a carrier of the tragic disease haemophilia, a disease which killed her son Leopold, and from which the Tsarevich Alexis suffered.*

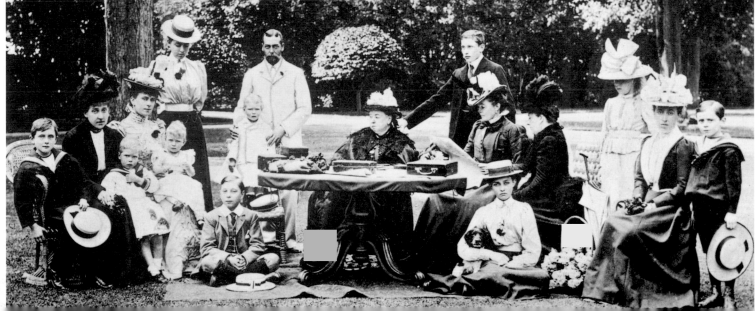

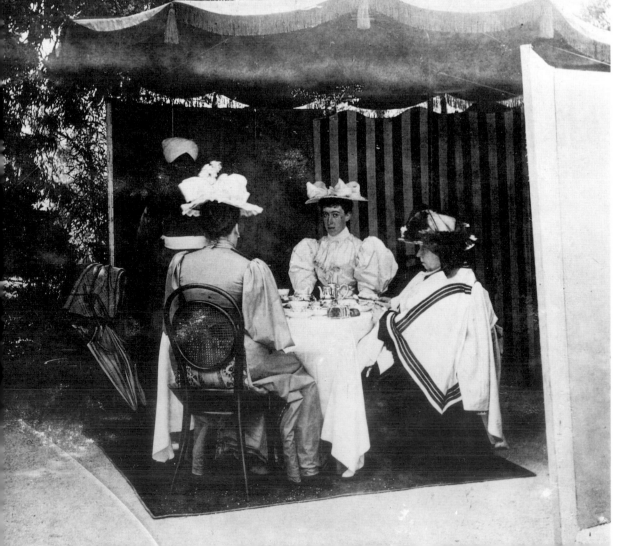

ABOVE, LEFT AND RIGHT: *As she grew older, Victoria's family became increasingly important to her. She is pictured above with the royal families of Germany, Russia and England in 1894; left with her daughters, the Princesses Beatrice and Victoria; and right with her grandchildren.*

ABOVE RIGHT AND FAR RIGHT: *Victoria received an ecstatic welcome in Ireland in 1900, but preferred to spend her time quietly, corresponding with her children, as this wax model at Madame Tussaud's illustrates.*

THESE PAGES: *The death of Victoria in 1901 brought to an end a reign lasting 63 years. She would be succeeded firstly by Edward VII (below left, standing left), and then by George V (standing right).*

No. 270.

Special Army Order.

SOUTH AFRICAN FIELD FORCE.

ARMY HEADQUARTERS,
PRETORIA.

24th January, 1901.

DEATH OF HER MAJESTY QUEEN VICTORIA—

The following telegram has been received from the Adjutant-General, War Office, dated London, 23rd January, 1901:—

"Commander-in-Chief deeply regrets to inform you of the death of Her Majesty Victoria, Queen of the United Kingdom of Great Britain and Ireland and of the Colonies and Dependencies thereof, Empress of India, who departed this life at 6-30 p.m., 22nd January, at Osborne House, Isle of Wight."

The following from Lord Kitchener has been sent in reply:

"The news of the Queen's death has been received with the greatest grief by the Army in South Africa. In their name I beg to express our sincere condolences with the Royal Family on the great loss sustained by them and the Nation."

By Order.

W. F. KELLY, Major-General.
Adjutant-General.

CHAPTER ONE

EDWARD VII
1901-10

If Queen Victoria established many of the modern monarchy's official functions, then her eldest son was the first to introduce some of the leisure pursuits that the royal family follow to this day, including horse racing, sailing and shooting. Edward VII was destined to spend most of his life waiting for the job of king. There is no official constitutional rôle for the Prince of Wales and his mother, doubtful of her eldest son's abilities and anxious to ensure that power remained firmly with her, denied her son access to even the most innocuous state papers. Prince Albert Edward (Bertie to his family) was forced, therefore, to find some alternative occupation and devoted the greater part of his adult life to the pursuit of pleasure.

The education of the young Prince of Wales was carefully planned by his exacting father Prince Albert, the Prince Consort, who sought to mould a mature, well-rounded constitutional monarch. He and the Queen took their responsibilities very seriously and were perhaps made more than usually anxious just three months after the birth of their eldest son by the well-meaning comment of an old advisor in 1841: 'The first truth by which the Queen and Prince ought to be thoroughly permeated is, that their position is a more difficult one than that of any other parents in the kingdom'.

Bertie spent his first few years in the shadow of his precocious elder sister, Victoria, the Princess Royal, and was shocked when he was told in 1852, at the age of 11, that it was he, not Vicky, who would one day succeed to the throne. He struggled under the pressure of his father's ambitious educational schemes, provoking frequent complaints in his mother's diary about his 'backwardness' or the need for 'improvement'. He was essentially a bright, affectionate child who was subjected to an unreasonable regime by a demanding father.

The Prince of Wales finished his formal education with brief periods at Oxford and Cambridge, and

finally 10 weeks of officer training with the Army at Curragh in Northern Ireland. Expected to pass qualifying exams for every rank from ensign to battalion commander, Bertie excelled himself by discovering the pleasures of the flesh in the arms of the actress Nellie Clifton. An enraged Prince Albert hurried to reprimand his son and caught a serious chill. When he died a few weeks later from typhoid, the Queen was convinced that his anxiety over Bertie had killed him, and her bitterness showed in her attitude to her son for many years.

Marriage was prescribed as a remedy for the wayward Prince of Wales, and in 1863 he married Princess Alexandra of Denmark, a beautiful and graceful 18-year-old. While the Queen continued to mourn for her departed husband, the Prince and Princess of Wales found themselves at the centre of London's smart set, where they became extremely popular. By the 1870s they had five children and had made their home in Marlborough House in London. The Prince built Sandringham House in Norfolk as their country retreat, and the couple lived the life of conventional Victorian aristocracy, doing the London 'season' and retreating to the country for house parties at weekends.

A man of considerable charm, the Prince appreciated beautiful women, and his mistresses were tolerated by his long-suffering wife, who turned a dignified blind eye on her husband's liaisons. Alexandra devoted herself to her children, who all adored their 'darling Motherdear', as they called her. The eldest son of the Prince and Princess of Wales, Prince Albert Victor (or Eddy to his family) was the only one to cause them any real concern. Brought up in a far more relaxed manner than his father, he nevertheless appeared mentally slow, even vacant. He was commissioned

RIGHT: *Edward VII poses for a formal portrait at the beginning of his reign.*

20

FAR LEFT AND LEFT: *Winterhalter's portrait of the seven-year-old Prince Albert Edward, and (left) the Prince aged 18.*

ABOVE: *Princess Alexandra of Denmark. The Queen and Prince Albert agonized over the choice of bride for Bertie, and much was expected of her. After their eldest son's escapades, the Queen wrote, 'I look to his wife as being his salvation'.*

into the Army, but was interested only in the uniforms and was unable to master even basic drill movements. Rumours of a dissipated private life shocked even his easy-going father, who worried about the state of the Crown in Eddy's hands. Prince Albert Victor's death in January 1892 was perceived as a national tragedy, and his family were devastated, but the nation probably had a lucky escape.

The Queen deplored Bertie's predilection for riotous house parties, gambling and racing, but his popularity with the people was undoubted. While the Queen rarely appeared in public, it was her eldest son who provided a focus for the nation's perpetual interest in the monarchy. In 1871 the Prince nearly died of typhoid, and the subsequent service of thanksgiving for his recovery produced a surge in public enthusiasm for the Prince of Wales himself, and for the monarchy as an institution. Despite repeated requests by government ministers to provide some sort of employment for her son, the Queen consistently refused to show him government dispatches, believing that he was too indiscreet to be trusted with even minor government secrets. It was not until 1892 that Lord Rosebery, the Foreign Secretary, presented the Prince of Wales with the Prince Consort's gold key, allowing him unrestricted access to official papers. The Prince of Wales fulfilled a comprehensive programme of official engagements, touring India in 1875 and

organizing the celebrations for his mother's Golden and Diamond Jubilees, but Queen Victoria made scant use of her son's diplomatic gifts and exceptional vitality, so he put them to use in a more hedonistic manner. There is no doubt that he found his position irksome, once commenting: 'I don't mind praying to the eternal father, but I must be the only man in the country afflicted with an eternal mother'.

The Prince of Wales finally came into his inheritance at the age of 59. King Edward VII's reign was characterized by a frenzy of diplomatic activity. Known as the 'uncle of Europe', he was closely related to many European sovereigns, including the German Kaiser, the King of Spain, the Tsar of Russia and the King of Norway, and put his family links to good use. Relations with France also improved after the King's state visit of 1903, although the Anglo-French *Entente Cordiale* was viewed with suspicion by Germany.

He interfered little in home affairs, although at the end of his reign the crisis provoked by the Liberal government over the power of the House of Lords nearly forced him to take a more active interest. The hot political issues of the day – suffragettes, the radical social reforms of Asquith's government, industrial problems – all seemed to pass him by. He was assiduous in dealing with his boxes of state papers but, when it came to domestic politics, he seemed content to follow the advice of his ministers and, unlike his

ABOVE: *The Prince and Princess of Wales on their wedding day.*

mother, did not proffer endless letters of advice and instruction.

Edward VII enjoyed only a short reign, but he gave his name to an age which still evokes an impression both of fun and of imperial pre-war stability. The rakish reputation he had earned as Prince of Wales was largely dispelled by his achievements between 1901 and 1910. It is probably true to say that, in the end, he fulfilled his father's ambitions for him and was a truly successful constitutional monarch.

LEFT, BELOW AND BOTTOM:
*Bertie and Alix embarked on
married life and quickly
produced a family – two boys
and three girls between 1864
and 1869.*

LEFT AND FAR LEFT: *The Prince
and Princess of Wales were
married in St George's Chapel
at Windsor Castle. Queen
Victoria got to know her future
daughter-in-law before the
engagement and liked her
immensely: 'such a jewel, whom
he [Bertie] is lucky to have
obtained', she wrote.*

BELOW: *The Prince of Wales in the late 1870s in Hussar uniform. Although the Prince shouldered many of his mother's official duties, he had no clearly-defined rôle in public life.*

ABOVE AND RIGHT: *Marital fidelity was not one of Bertie's virtues and his wife bore his philandering philosophically, devoting much of her time to her children. The Prince and Princess are seen at right with Prince George, Prince Albert Victor and Princess Louise; above, Alexandra and her children in 1875, the ranks increased by the addition of Princesses Maud and Victoria.*

ABOVE RIGHT: *In 1875 the Prince and Princess of Wales visited the Suez Canal shortly before it opened. The Prince went on to make a triumphant tour of India.*

RIGHT: *The visit of the Shah of Persia, 1873. Throughout his mother's reign, Edward VII put his considerable charm to good use in the field of diplomatic relations.*

THESE PAGES: *A genial man who was self-assured and charming, the Prince of Wales possessed a strong hedonistic streak. Throughout his adult life he lacked any real intellectual challenges – indeed, he was* *averse to reading, desk work or the arts. The pace of his life was frenetic, filled with a selection of minor public duties, but principally dominated by house parties, balls, and racing.*

TOP: *A shooting party in Derry Lodge, Scotland, 1891. The Prince and Princess of Wales are accompanied by their sons, Prince George (second left) and Prince Albert Victor (fourth left).*

ABOVE: *The Goodwood house party of 1866; the Prince is seated second left, his wife fourth left.*

ABOVE: *The Wales family in 1889. Left to right: the Duke of Clarence, Princess Maud (later Queen of Norway), Princess Alexandra, Princess Louise, Duchess of Fife, Prince Albert Edward. Seated are Prince George (later George V) and Princess Victoria. As her children grew older, Princess Alexandra appeared evermore youthful. She had a tenacious, even clinging relationship with all of them, writing them letters in a childish language. Increasingly deaf, she relied on her family for amusement.*

LEFT: *The Prince of Wales with his sons Prince Albert Victor, Duke of Clarence and Prince George. The death of Prince Albert Victor in February 1891 at the age of 27 devastated the family, but he was a curiously slow and ineffectual young man who would not have made an ideal king. Interested only in women and uniforms, 'Eddy's' demise was a family tragedy, but perhaps a blessing in disguise for the nation.*

RIGHT: *Sir Max Beerbohm's cartoon:* The rare the rather awful visits of Albert Edward, Prince of Wales, to Windsor Castle.

LEFT AND RIGHT: *Edward VII acceded to the throne on 22 January 1901, aged 59. Fascinated by uniforms, ceremonial and protocol, he was a stickler for formality, and plans for his coronation absorbed a great deal of his attention during 1901. A serious attack of appendicitis in June 1902 forced the whole event to be abandoned at the last minute, however. The King underwent an appendectomy in Buckingham Palace and, despite fears for his life, made an astonishing recovery, giving the nation double cause for rejoicing when the coronation finally took place three months later.*

BELOW: *A souvenir postcard showing Edward VII and Queen Alexandra surrounded by various illustrious relations. Clockwise from top left: the Prince and Princess of Wales; the King's daughter Queen Maud and her husband Haakon VII of Norway; the King's nephew Kaiser Wilhelm II of Germany and the Kaiserin Augusta; the King's niece Queen Eugenie with her husband Alfonso XIII of Spain.*

RIGHT: *The royal families of Britain and Russia, 1908. Queen Alexandra was the sister of the Tsar's mother, which may account for the astonishing physical resemblance between Tsar Nicholas II (seated second left) and his cousin George, Prince of Wales (seated second right).*

RIGHT: *A family group c1895. The Duke of York (later George V) with his eldest son (later Edward VIII) on his knee.*

THIS PAGE: *Edward VII enjoyed a close relationship with his son Prince George. In 1901 the Duke and Duchess of York departed on a six-month tour of Australia, leaving their children (above right) with their indulgent grandparents. The Duke and Duchess seemed to cope with the prospect of a long absence with equanimity, but King Edward could barely hold back his tears at their farewell banquet on 16 March 1901.*

35

THIS PAGE: *One of Edward VII's more concrete legacies was the* Entente Cordiale *with France. A life-long Francophile, the King's state visit in 1903 was a tremendous success. He was a natural diplomat and was anxious to strengthen the ties between the two countries, as his corrections to the draft speech (below) show.*

Copy

The King's Speech àt the Hôtel de Ville, 2/5/03.

" Je désire vous exprimer combien je suis vivement "touché de vos bonnes paroles. Il aurait été fâcheux, en .passant par votre belle ville, de ne pouvoir m'arrêter ~~un moment~~ à l'Hôtel de Ville. Bien sincèrement, je vous "remercie de l'accueil que vous m'avez fait aujourd'hui. "Je n'oublierai ~~pas~~ *jamais* ma visite à votre charmante ville "et je puis vous assurer que c'est avec le plus grand *à Paris, où je me trouve toujours* "plaisir que je reviens ~~parmi vous, car j'ai l'impression~~ ~~d'être à Paris comme dans mon propre pays~~".

comme si j'étais chez moi.

ABOVE: *King Edward (seated left) and Queen Alexandra (standing off-centre), surrounded by various European relatives.*

LEFT: *King Edward with his nephew Kaiser Wilhelm II of Germany in Berlin, 1909. Family ties with the German Empire were closer than diplomatic ones during the King's reign. His nephew was a bellicose and ambitious monarch intent on building up German military, naval and imperial might. Furthermore, he was deeply suspicious of the Anglo-French* Entente, *which he believed was designed to isolate Germany.*

THIS PAGE: *Affairs of state did not interrupt the King's social life. A keen horseman, shot and sailor, he enjoyed outdoor pursuits. The purchase of the Sandringham estate in Norfolk when he was Prince of Wales provided him with the ideal venue for shooting weekends.*

LEFT: *Horse racing is still known as the 'sport of kings', largely because of Edward VII's interest.*

BELOW: *Fascinated by new gadgetry and inventions, Edward purchased a 'horseless carriage' in 1901. He is seen here in 1899 with Mr Montagu who was asked to demonstrate his Daimler. Queen Alexandra was also keen on motoring, though perhaps not an ideal passenger, writing that 'I poke him [the chauffeur] violently in the back at every corner to go gently'.*

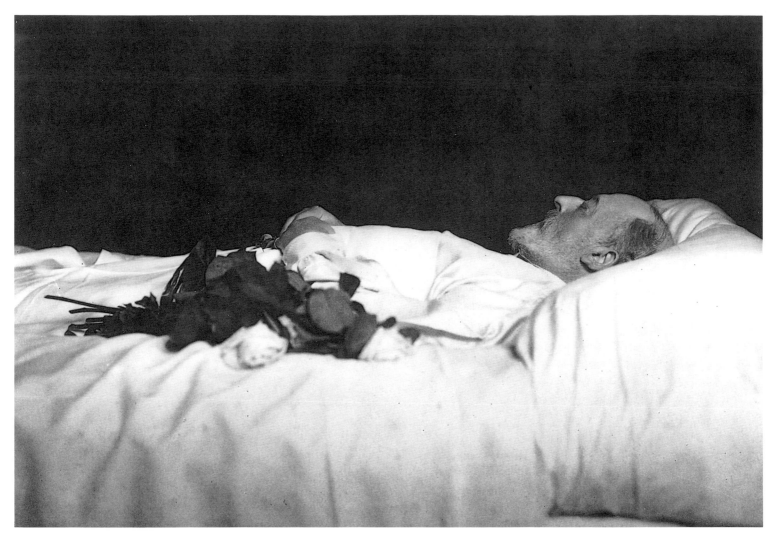

ABOVE: *Queen Alexandra outlived her husband by 15 years. She died in 1925 at the age of 81.*

ABOVE LEFT, LEFT, ABOVE,
AND RIGHT: *Edward VII died
in May 1910 after a series of
bronchial attacks which his
regular visits to the spas of
France and Germany did little
to alleviate. His funeral later
that month was attended by
many of the crowned heads of
Europe (above), a fitting and
dignified tribute.*

41

CHAPTER TWO

GEORGE V
1910-36

George V's reign was not an outstandingly long one, but his life joined the nineteenth century to the twentieth. Lord Palmerston, that veteran of nineteenth-century foreign politics, was present at his christening in 1865; shortly before he died in 1936, the seals of the Foreign Office were passed to Anthony Eden. A quiet, naturally conservative man, George V reigned during one of the most troubled periods of twentieth-century history, encompassing World War I and severe economic depression. As king, he faced most of the problems of government with robust pragmatism, bringing to bear a sound judgement unimpeded by prejudice or condescension. He seemed to grow into the rôle of king, and by the end of his reign was regarded with respect and affection throughout the Empire.

Born in 1865, Prince George Frederick Ernest Albert was not destined for the throne. He was the second son of the young Prince and Princess of Wales, and was brought up in a far more relaxed manner than his father. His brother, Prince Albert Victor, was only 18 months older, and the young princes were educated together. To the slight dismay of their tutors and parents, it was evident that Prince George was not only more intelligent than his brother but, more to the point, was actually receptive to learning. Eddy (as the royal family called Prince Albert Victor) was distinctly listless and slow; their tutor, the Reverend Dalton, noted that 'Prince Albert Victor requires the stimulus of Prince George's company to induce him to work at all . . . Prince George's lively presence is his mainstay and chief incentive to exertion . . . ' The two princes were sent to sea in 1879 (accompanied by Mr Dalton) on a three-year voyage. Three years on board a warship was an exacting education, and the two princes enjoyed few privileges, experiencing all the rigours of naval life.

A naval career was considered entirely suitable for the second son of the Heir Apparent, and Prince George continued on active service until 1893. It was envisaged that he would continue to enjoy country pursuits while on leave, (he was a crack shot all his life) and in the fullness of time marry a suitable princess or well-born Englishwoman. His life, in other words, would be comfortable and relatively undemanding. Prince George's destiny changed forever in January 1892, however, when his elder brother caught a cold. Eddy developed inflammation of the lungs and on 14 January 1892 he died. Devoted to his brother, Prince George was devastated by the death, and horrified by his own changed circumstances. He was quickly fitted out with the provisions necessary for his new status – two households, a dukedom and a greatly increased income – but he lacked the final, vital ingredient: a wife.

Prince Albert Victor had shown a tendency to fall in love with unsuitable women, and in 1891 the royal family recognized the need for, in the words of the Prince of Wales, 'a good sensible wife with some considerable character' to keep the wayward heir in order. The spotlight had fallen on Princess May of Teck, whose mother was Queen Victoria's cousin. Intelligent and sensible, she became engaged to Eddy in December and the wedding was planned, with almost unseemly haste, for the following February. History does not record whether she perceived the death of her fiancé as a blessed relief or an incomparable tragedy, but she survived this crisis, as she was to surmount every crisis in her life, with dignity and courage. Keenly aware of Princess May's virtues, the royal family were anxious not to lose her and encouraged Prince George to fill his brother's shoes in one last way.

The courtship of Prince George and Princess May was short and the couple were both crippled by

RIGHT: *George V in 1906, when he was Prince of Wales.*

ABOVE, FAR LEFT: *Prince George and his sisters on board the royal yacht.*

ABOVE LEFT: *The Teck family c1885. Princess May is seated (right) with her brothers and her mother.*

FAR LEFT: *Princess May of Teck shortly before her engagement to Prince George's elder brother. The Tecks were cousins of the royal family, Princess May's mother being a first cousin of Queen Victoria.*

LEFT: *Prince George, Duke of York with his cousin, Nicholas II of Russia (seated). 'Exactly like a skinny Duke of York – the image of him' wrote Queen Victoria in 1896.*

ABOVE: *The wedding of Princess May of Teck and Prince George, Duke of York.*

LEFT: *The happy couple pose with the Prince's grandmother, Queen Victoria. Originally intended as the bride of the wayward Prince Albert Victor, the royal family saw the marriage of Prince George to his dead brother's fiancée as an ideal solution to private grief and dynastic need. The young couple seemed extremely shy with each other, but their letters show rather more affection: 'It is so stupid to be so stiff together and really there is nothing I would not tell you, except that I love you more than anybody in the world . . .' wrote Princess May in 1893.*

RIGHT: *Immediately after their marriage the young Duke and Duchess of York moved into York Cottage on the Sandringham estate, and it became their home for the next 33 years. The Prince enjoyed the life of a country squire and Sandringham remained his favourite residence throughout his life.*

ABOVE: *The Duke of York with his eldest son, Prince Edward. As his children grew up they came to fear him as a stern and often brusque parent but, early in his marriage, Prince George boasted of his skill in bathing his son and settling down to an evening of peaceful domesticity with his wife.*

LEFT: *May in 1906 as Princess of Wales. An intelligent but reserved woman, her in-laws did not always understand her. She was uneasy at large social gatherings and her shyness was mistaken for arrogance. Queen Victoria's private secretary wrote in 1894 'She is pretty and what you would call voluptuous, but decidedly dull'.*

ABOVE LEFT: *(from left) Prince Edward, the ill-fated Nicholas II of Russia, his son the Tsarevich Alexis, and George, Prince of Wales in 1909.*

ABOVE: *The Wales family in 1902. From left: Prince Albert (later George VI), Princess Mary, Prince Edward (later Edward VIII) and Prince Henry, with their father.*

ABOVE: *The Prince and Princess of Wales with Prince Edward and Princess Victoria (left), the Prince's favourite sister, 1907.*

LEFT: *The complete Wales family, 1906. George V has acquired a reputation as a bad parent, his views on child-rearing allegedly summed up in his comment 'My father was frightened of his mother, I was frightened of my father and I'm damned well going to see that my children are frightened of me'.*

RIGHT AND LEFT: *George V and Queen Mary at the time of their accession in 1910. A slight man, George V made the most of his natural attributes. He was always dressed immaculately and was almost obsessive about his appearance and that of those around him. His conservative tastes were impressed on his wife. Queen Mary's dignified and almost unchanging appearance throughout her husband's reign is directly attributable to the King. After World War I, the Queen thought she might raise her skirt hems an inch or two to show her ankles. She persuaded a lady-in-waiting to act as guinea pig to gauge the King's reaction, which was unfavourable. Queen Mary's skirts consequently remained rooted almost to the ground until 1936.*

LEFT: *When George V became King, he also became Emperor of India, and was determined to visit the subcontinent. In November 1911 the King and Queen set off for Bombay, the first King-Emperor to receive the homage of millions of Indian subjects in their homeland. His visit culminated in the magnificent Delhi Durbar, one of the most impressive spectacles in the history of the British Empire.*

LEFT AND BELOW: *George V with his cousin, Kaiser Wilhelm II, during a visit to Germany in 1913. Close family ties were not enough to change the Kaiser's view that British foreign policy was anti-German.*

LEFT: *On 22 June 1911 George V was crowned in Westminster Abbey. He wrote in his diary 'The Service in the Abbey was most beautiful and impressive, but it was a terrible ordeal'. The Queen echoed his words, noting '. . . it was an awful ordeal for us both, especially as we felt it all so deeply and taking so great a responsibility on our shoulders . . .'*

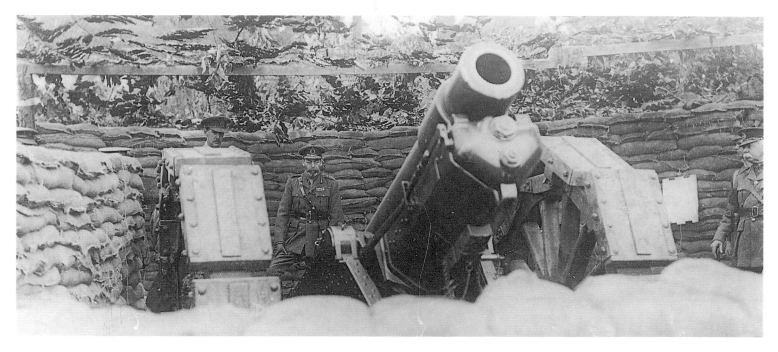

THESE PAGES: *During the Great War, the King did everything he could to encourage his ministers and fighting men. He struggled to preserve everyday decencies. Contemptuous of the Germans' bombing of civilian targets in Zeppelin raids, he hated the idea of similar reprisals, wishing to conduct the war 'as far as possible with humanity and like gentlemen'. From 1914 to 1918 he paid 450 visits to troops, 300 to hospitals, and almost as many to industrial complexes. He fell from his horse during a visit to the Western Front in 1915, cracking three ribs and fracturing his pelvis. The nation was overwhelmed by phobia of all things German, and by 1917 the King had given in to a whispering campaign against his family's Germanic origins and changed the name of his dynasty from Saxe-Coburg-Gotha to Windsor.*

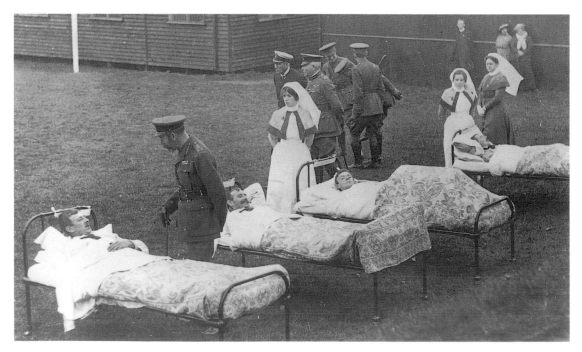

ABOVE: *The royal family in the early 1920s. From left: Edward, Prince of Wales; Princess Mary; Henry, Duke of Gloucester; King George V; Albert, Duke of York; Queen Mary; George, Duke of Kent.*

RIGHT: *The Duke of Kent and Queen Mary with the newly-wed Duke and Duchess of York in 1923 at Balmoral. Queen Mary was devoted to her children, but her affection was tempered by the fact that, as she said: 'I always have to remember that their father is also their king'.*

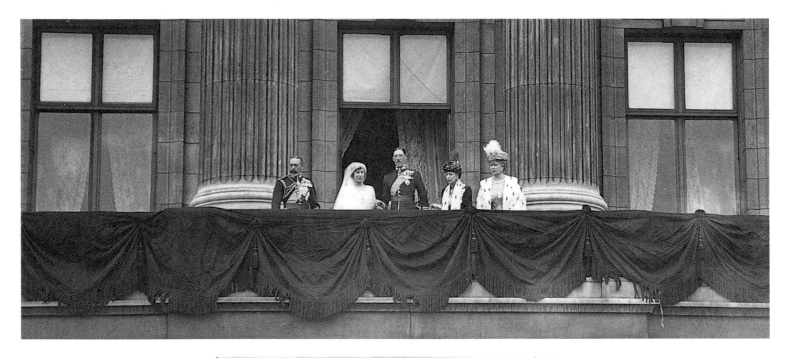

RIGHT: *The King with the Prince of Wales in 1928. George V did not enjoy an easy relationship with his eldest son. A conservative man, he found little to sympathize with in what he regarded as his son's racy lifestyle, and Prince Edward, like so many veterans of World War I, sought a relaxation of the strict conventions of his upbringing. When Lord Mountbatten's father died, the Prince of Wales provided rather chilling words of comfort: 'I envy you a father whom you could love. If my father had died, we should have felt nothing but relief'.*

ABOVE: *The marriage of the Princess Mary to Viscount Lascelles in May 1922. The King was reluctant to see his only daughter leave the family circle, and her brothers were unimpressed by Lascelles, a man 15 years her senior. He was, however, an exceedingly rich landowner, with extensive estates in Yorkshire. The couple had two sons and shared a passion for horses and racing. Created Princess Royal in 1932, Princess Mary dreaded public engagements, but fulfilled a crowded calendar.*

THESE PAGES: *Shooting was the King's first love (right: with his shooting pony, Jock), but he was also an accomplished sailor. His yacht* Britannia *had been commissioned for his father; George V re-rigged it as a racing cruiser in 1913 and* launched it on an immensely successful racing career. The annual sailing at Cowes Week provided him with a complete release from affairs of state, and it was a hobby he enjoyed until his death.

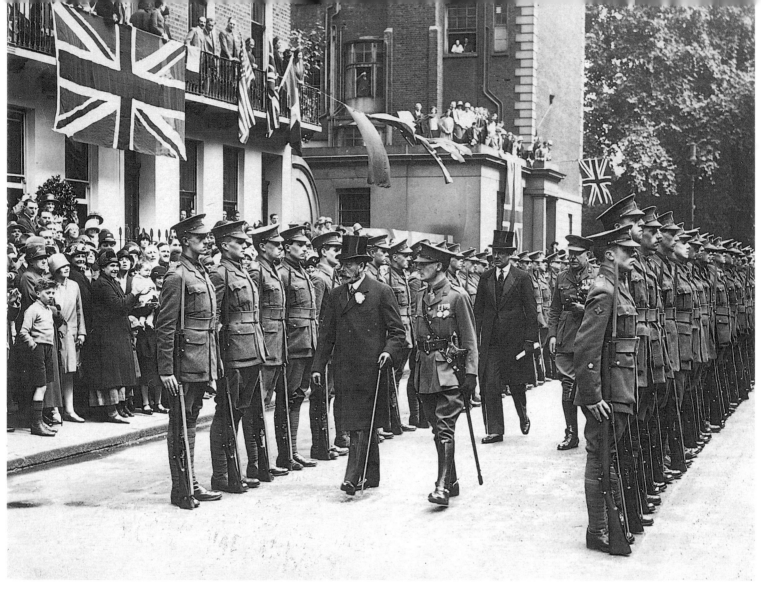

ABOVE, ABOVE RIGHT, AND RIGHT: *George V's life operated according to a rigid timetable of state and social occasions. The early summer was spent in London, hosting garden parties at Buckingham Palace, attending Ascot and the annual Garter Ceremony at Windsor.*

OPPOSITE PAGE, ABOVE AND BELOW: *After World War I the royal family made a conscious effort to become more accessible. An increasing number of official engagements were in industrial working-class areas. They also opened exhibitions that promoted Britain and the Empire, such as the Wembley Exhibition, 1925 (below left).*

LEFT: *George V with the colonial prime ministers in 1926. A conscientious imperial monarch, George V nevertheless hated foreign travel and preferred to send his sons to his dominions as his representatives.*

THESE PAGES: *In November 1928 the 63-year-old King became seriously ill with a bronchial infection. A medical bulletin warily mentioned 'a decline of strength in the heart' and the Prince of Wales was summoned home from a safari in East Africa. The country was prepared for the worst, but George V survived. He spent the early months of 1929 convalescing in Bognor, and only returned home to Sandringham in March.*

ABOVE: *Queen Mary in the early days of widowhood. A keen needlewoman, she taught all her sons the art of petit point.*

RIGHT: *Queen Mary opening the new dock at Southampton, 1933. She sacrificed her life to public duty, believing that her primary role was to safeguard the health and happiness of the King. After his death, she found more time to indulge her own interests.*

ABOVE: *The wedding of the King's third son, Henry, Duke of Gloucester in 1935. Left to right: Princess Elizabeth, King George, Princess Margaret, Princess Mary, the Princess Royal, the Duke and Duchess of Gloucester, Queen Mary.*

RIGHT: *Known for her love of fine antiques and china, Queen Mary is seen here rather uncharacteristically clutching a mug of tea during a visit to a YMCA canteen in 1942.*

BELOW: *Queen Mary and the Prince of Wales during a garden party at Buckingham Palace, 1935.*

RIGHT: *On 6 May 1935 Britain celebrated the Silver Jubilee of George V and Queen Mary. 'I remember so well both Queen Victoria's Jubilees', wrote the King, 'and can't yet realize that I am having one now.' The pragmatic government grabbed the opportunity for a display of national affection, and although the King was horrified by the expense, he was touched by the response.*

LEFT AND RIGHT: *The King and Queen drove to St Paul's Cathedral with their family for the Thanksgiving Service, through streets lined with cheering crowds: 'the greatest number of people in the streets that I have ever seen in my life', noted the King.*

RIGHT: *The King presents the Football Association Trophy to the captain of Manchester City at Wembley, 1935. In the last year of his life, 70-year-old George V became tired and ill. Although overwhelmed by the response to his Jubilee, it weakened his health.*

BELOW: *The first British monarch to speak to his people on the wireless, George V broadcast his first Christmas message in 1934. It was extremely well received, although the King himself found it rather trying and complained that it spoilt his Christmas.*

RIGHT AND BELOW: *George V died at Sandringham on 20 January 1936. His body was taken to Westminster, where it lay in state prior to his funeral (right). His sons followed the gun carriage bearing their father's coffin on foot (below), and on 27 January 1936 George V was interred in St George's Chapel, Windsor Castle.*

CHAPTER THREE
EDWARD VIII
1936

Prince Edward of York was born on 23 June 1894 at the height of Britain's imperial power, into a royal family that had never appeared more stable. With his great-grandmother still on the throne, the birth of the young Prince assured the succession into the third generation. It was thus ironic that after such a confident start Prince Edward, of all people, should be the individual who rocked the stability of the British monarchy to its core and came closest to upsetting the constitutional apple cart.

Christened Edward Albert Christian George Andrew Patrick David, he was known to his family as David. The nation rejoiced at his birth, the only discordant note being sounded by Keir Hardie, who gloomily commented: 'From his childhood onwards this boy will be surrounded by sycophants and flatterers by the score . . . A line will be drawn between him and the people he is to be called upon some day to reign over. In due course he will be sent on a tour round the world, and probably rumours of a morganatic alliance will follow, and the end of it will be the country is called upon to pay the bill'. Hardie never knew how accurate his words would be.

The young Prince had every advantage – wealth, good looks and doting, if diffident, parents. He was educated in the well-tested traditions of his family, that is by private tutors and at the Royal Naval College at Osborne and Dartmouth. His father, the Duke of York (later George V) was a strict disciplinarian and, although he doted on his children when they were toddlers, as they grew older he made it clear that he expected high standards of behaviour from them all, particularly his eldest son. A resentful Duke of Windsor wrote many years later: 'Kings and Queens are only secondarily fathers and mothers'. Queen Mary loved her children but treated them like small adults and seemed surprised when they were naughty or fractious. The children of George V and Queen Mary had a traditional Victorian upbringing; everyday care was left to nannies of varying degrees of competence and, as their parents only saw them for a couple of hours each day, they failed to notice that one nurse was bullying their eldest son and ruining the digestive system of another. Queen Mary was endowed with an admirable sense of duty but it did not make her the warmest of mothers. 'I always have to remember', she said of her sons,' that their father is also their king'.

In 1911, a year after his father's accession, Prince Edward was invested as Prince of Wales at Caernarvon Castle and won the hearts of the Welsh people with the few words of Welsh that Lloyd George had taught him. He became an undergraduate at Magdalen College, Oxford, in 1912 and thoroughly enjoyed the social life, but was less diligent with his studies. One report to his father began: 'Bookish he will never be'; in later life it is alleged that when a companion was discussing Graham Greene, the Prince thought he was talking about golf courses. Prince Edward left Oxford to join the Army and remained as a serving officer for the duration of World War I. He was given a commission in the Grenadier Guards, despite being five inches under the regulation height of six foot. Initially confined to duties in London, the Prince was eventually sent to France to serve on General French's staff. He deplored the fact that he was kept well away from front-line action, remarking that there were four brothers to take his place if he were killed.

He was barely given a chance to recover from the war when, in 1919, he was sent on the first of the foreign tours which won him popularity and acclaim throughout the Empire, but which Prince Edward found paralysingly boring. He went to Canada in 1919, Australia and New Zealand in 1920, and India in 1921.

RIGHT: *The Duke of Windsor, briefly King Edward VIII, with his duchess, the woman for whom he surrendered a throne.*

70

The strain of several months' continual travelling began to show in Australia, where he came close to collapse. By 1925 he had added South Africa and another North American tour to the list, and was finally allowed to settle in his home country.

The question of the Prince of Wales' marriage was one that had taxed his parents for several years. Quite how they expected him to find a suitable bride while travelling to all four corners of the Empire is a moot point, but it is true to say that the Prince himself showed no signs of wanting to settle down. He carried on discreet affairs with a number of married women, the longest of these being with Freda Dudley Ward and Thelma, Lady Furness. In 1931 Prince Edward was introduced to Wallis Simpson, the American wife of businessman Ernest Simpson. They met occasionally at parties in 1932 and, as she later put it, their relationship 'imperceptibly but swiftly passed from an acquaintanceship to a friendship'. By 1934 it was clear

that the Prince was infatuated with her; moreover he had completely severed relations with Mrs Dudley Ward and Lady Furness.

The Prince's behaviour did not escape the notice – and censure – of his parents who, not surprisingly, deplored their eldest son's association with an American divorcée. King George remarked to a friend: 'I pray to God that my eldest son will never marry and have children, and that nothing will come between Bertie and Lilibet [the Duke of York and Princess Elizabeth] and the throne'.

George V died on 20 January 1936 and his eldest son's reaction was one of almost hysterical grief. His family were surprised and attributed it to a rather belated sense of guilt after years of being at odds with his father. Many people looked to the new king to modernize the monarchy, and Edward did not disappoint them. He was impatient of excessive ceremony and cut back on Court expenditure. He was also extremely diligent to begin with, initialling all state papers that came his way. However, it was not long before Whitehall officials noticed that documents were not only returning to them slowly, but were often stained with circular marks left by cocktail glasses. The King insisted on living in Fort Belvedere, his private retreat in Windsor Great Park, merely keeping an office at Buckingham Palace, and officials found it difficult to contact him. He did not like being disturbed by official business when he was at the Fort and his courtiers could only visit by invitation. Furthermore, it was becoming clear that his infatuation with Mrs Simpson was waxing, not waning as many had hoped.

In the summer of 1936 the King hired a yacht for a cruise around the Mediterranean. He was photographed everywhere, always in the company of Mrs Simpson, whose husband was conspicuous by his absence. British newspapers discreetly painted Mrs Simpson out of the photos but the European and American press were less restrained, and cuttings from foreign papers were seen by Queen Mary as well as by government ministers. Mrs Simpson enjoyed flaunting her control over the King, who adopted an air of dog-like devotion in his beloved's presence. In September Mrs Simpson was granted a divorce and the prime minister, Stanley Baldwin, realized that the abdication of the King was a very real possibility.

Finally, on 16 November, the King told his prime minister that he intended to marry Mrs Simpson, despite the fact that, as a twice-divorced woman, she was not considered a suitable candidate for the position of Queen of England. As the diarist Chips Channon wrote: 'The country, or much of it, would not accept Queen Wallis with two live husbands scattered about'. The monarch is Supreme Governor of the Church of England and the Church did not allow

LEFT: *A rather pensive portrait of the Duke of Windsor shortly before his wedding in 1937.*

marriage between divorced persons. Various solutions were suggested, the principal one being a morganatic marriage whereby Mrs Simpson would become Edward VIII's wife but not queen. On 2 December the silence of the British press was shattered, and public opinion clearly indicated a disinclination to consider Mrs Simpson as queen. Both the King and Mrs Simpson were shocked: 'They don't want me', he said sadly, as he faced public censure for the first time in his life. He may have thought that his immense public popularity could have saved him.

Edward informed his brothers of his decision at the end of November and finally abdicated on 10 December 1936 after 350 days as king. He insisted on making a farewell broadcast to the country and this immediately focused attention on what his new title was to be. In the last days before his abdication and departure for exile in France, Edward was preoccupied with both titles and money, and for months afterwards

bombarded George VI with phone calls and letters on the subject. He was eventually styled, 'His Royal Highness Prince Edward, Duke of Windsor', but his wife was denied the epithet 'Royal Highness', which was perceived as a slur by the Duke and soured his relationship with the royal family for the rest of his life.

Exiled and unemployed, the Duke of Windsor cut a pathetic figure. During World War II he was the focus of Nazi attention, as Hitler believed him to be sympathetic to Germany's cause and intended to reinstate him when the Germans invaded Britain. The Duke longed for some sort of official job, which was ironic considering his life-long loathing of public duties. He intended to return to live in England, but both the government and his brother George VI discouraged this movement and he remained in exile until he died. He always maintained that: 'I acted in good faith. And I was treated bloody shabbily'.

ABOVE AND RIGHT: *The young Prince Edward of York seen above with his great-grandmother, Queen Victoria, c1896 and, right, c1900.*

THIS PAGE: *After the death of his grandfather, Edward VII (seated above), the 16-year-old Prince Edward became Prince of Wales. In 1911, with the Prince dressed in what he called a 'preposterous rig', top right, a formal investiture ceremony was held at Caernarvon Castle, top left, the first for 300 years. He is seen, right, in Garter robes.*

C 6973

TOP, ABOVE AND LEFT: *When the Great War broke out in 1914, the 20-year-old Prince was anxious to join the Grenadier Guards. He was sent to a 'safe' job on the staff of General French, well away from the front line, and deplored the fact that he was kept away from the fighting.*

THESE PAGES: *In 1919 the Prince of Wales was sent to Canada and the United States on the first of several gruelling foreign tours that were to occupy much of his time in the 1920s. He was the first heir to the throne to visit just about the entire Empire. Although he found parts of the tours stultifyingly boring, he was extremely popular, and was mobbed. 'You just can't think how enthusiastic the crowds have been', he wrote to his father from Canada.*

THIS PAGE: *Prince Edward found time for relaxation between tours. He enjoyed hunting, racing and golf, among other sports.*

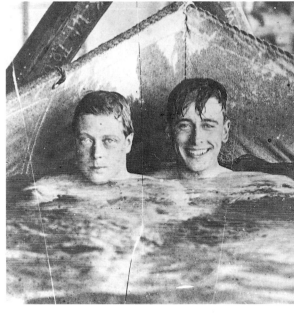

THIS PAGE: *The Prince of Wales' second major tour was to Australia and New Zealand in 1920. He is seen above on board* HMS Renown *with his cousin, Lord Louis Mountbatten, who accompanied him.*

RIGHT: *The Prince of Wales with his staff at Federal Government House, Melbourne, during his 1920 tour. He had only three months in England between his return from Canada and his departure for Australia and, by the end of his time in Australia, it became clear that he was close to a breakdown.*

ABOVE: *By the 1930s, the Prince of Wales was being allowed to remain in Britain, and carried out official duties nearer to home.*

RIGHT: *Prince Edward with his younger brother, Prince George, Duke of Kent (centre) during naval exercises in the Mediterranean, 1932.*

LEFT; TOP, MIDDLE AND BOTTOM: *Although he found many of his official functions boring, the Prince relished meeting his future subjects. He was struck by the appalling conditions in which many of them lived, and was amazed, he wrote to Stanley Baldwin (top, second left) that they 'weren't at all complaining, seemed glad to see one, and only told of their troubles when asked'.*

BELOW: *The Prince of Wales chatting to Mrs Simpson at Ascot, 1935.*

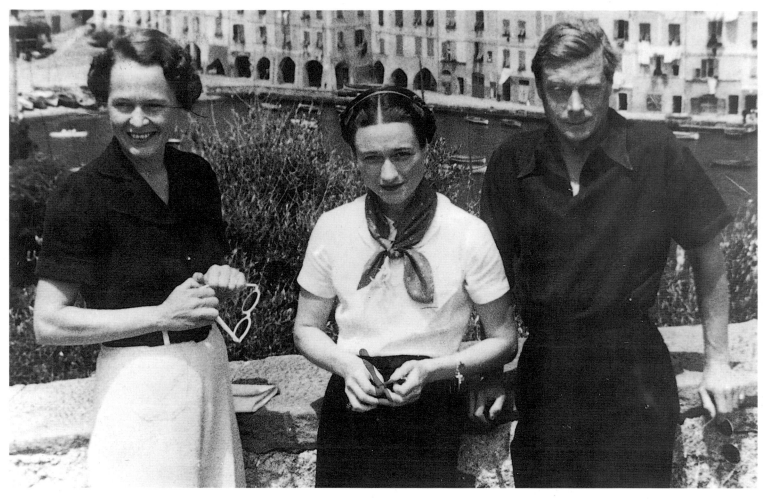

THESE PAGES: *By the time of his accession to the throne in January 1936, Edward's relationship with the American divorcée Wallis Simpson was an open secret in royal circles. Their affair probably began in 1934, despite the existence of her husband, who seemed happy with the reflected glory of his wife's royal connections. The royal family, however, regarded her as a charmless, ruthless social climber. They believed she was the Prince's mistress and George V was reluctant to receive her at Court. She was the only woman who made Prince Edward happy, and when he became king he was determined not to lose her.*

ABOVE AND LEFT: *The Duke died aged 75, of throat cancer, on 27 May 1972. His body was flown to Britain and lay in state in St George's Chapel. It was only when Garter King of Arms got to the end of the Duke's long list of heraldic honours that the congregation realized how much he had sacrificed – 'one-time King Edward VIII of Great Britain, Ireland and the British Dominions beyond the Seas, Emperor of India'.*

ABOVE AND RIGHT: *For nearly 40 years the Duke and Duchess of Windsor had appeared inseparable. Alone in public for the first time, at her husband's funeral, the Duchess had never seemed so isolated.*

CHAPTER FOUR
GEORGE VI
1937-52

Prince Albert of York was born on an ill-fated day, 14 December 1895, the anniversary of the Prince Consort's death, and was not destined or educated to be king. After his elder brother's abdication, however, he emerged as a popular, dutiful and successful monarch who earned the country's respect for his leadership and example during World War II. He could have moved his family to Canada or at least to Scotland in 1940, but chose instead to remain in London and endure the Blitz with his people. This determination to share the experiences, and to a certain extent the suffering, of the country aroused immense admiration in the hearts of Britons, and Londoners in particular.

As a second son, Prince Albert (or Bertie as he was known to his family) was not subject to the same pressures as his elder brother, Prince Edward. His childhood was blighted, however, by a vindictive nanny, who dented his self-confidence to such an extent that he suffered from a noticeable stammer all his life. He suffered from gastric problems and had to wear painful splints for his knock-knees, and it is not really surprising that he seemed overshadowed by his elder brother. He followed Prince Edward to Osborne and Dartmouth, where he distinguished himself by remaining at the bottom of the class. He learned to play tennis at Dartmouth and became extremely skilful, particularly when the masters encouraged him to follow his natural inclination to use his left hand. He remains the only member of the royal family to have competed in the Wimbledon tennis championships.

The traditional career for the monarch's second son was the Navy, and in 1913 Prince Albert embarked on his cadet training on the cruiser *Cumberland*. It was unfortunate that the Prince should suffer from sea-sickness, but he saw action at the Battle of Jutland in 1916 despite suffering from a painful duodenal ulcer. He spent the last months of the war in the Royal Naval Air Service and then in the newly-inaugurated Royal Air Force, where he became the first member of the royal family to qualify as a pilot. His mother, Queen Mary, ever-conscious of the precedent of second sons succeeding to the throne, had long urged that Prince Albert 'ought to be educated also', and in 1919 he finished his formal education with a short spell at Cambridge, studying constitutional history with his younger brother, Prince Henry.

While the glamorous Prince of Wales was sent round the world to show Britain's gratitude to the Empire for its support during the war, Prince Albert was enlisted for the more mundane task of showing the face of the royal family to the ordinary people of Britain. Created Duke of York in 1920, he lived with his parents in Buckingham Palace during the early 1920s, carrying out public duties and grappling with his stammer whenever he was called upon to make a speech. His elder brother made infrequent but heavily-publicized trips to areas of urban and industrial decay, but the Duke of York worked unobtrusively for years as President of the Industrial Welfare Society to improve the lot of young workers, and in 1921 instituted the Duke of York's Camp, a holiday camp for boys from all backgrounds. It was an imaginative and innovative idea simply because it was the first scheme successfully to mix boys from different backgrounds.

In 1923, after three proposals, Prince Albert finally persuaded Lady Elizabeth Bowes-Lyon to be his wife. She was a beautiful and vivacious young woman and the Duke of York was not her only suitor. He was the most persistent, however, and it was only with great tenacity that he persuaded her to abandon her carefree private existence and embrace the public duties and restricted lifestyle of the royal family. She could not

RIGHT: *George VI presents new regimental colours to the Grenadier Guards, 1938.*

RIGHT: *The royal family at Buckingham Palace, 1942.*

LEFT: *George VI at the Royal Lodge, Windsor, 1946. The war has clearly taken its toll; a year after the end of hostilities, he looks gaunt and drawn.*

have known then quite what the future would hold.

Having confided to Queen Mary that he dreaded the idea of having daughters-in-law, George V was enchanted by Bertie's wife. After their marriage in 1923, the Duke and Duchess settled down to quiet domesticity at 145 Piccadilly and it was here that their first child, Princess Elizabeth, was born in 1926. The influence of the Duchess on Prince Albert was paramount; he blossomed in her presence and, more practically, she encouraged him to consult the speech therapist, Lionel Logue, who effected a considerable improvement on the Prince's speech.

In 1927 the Duke and Duchess embarked on a six-month visit to Australia, leaving the infant Princess Elizabeth with her grandparents. 'I felt very much

leaving on Thursday', wrote the Duchess, 'and the baby was so sweet playing with the buttons on Bertie's uniform that it quite broke me up'. The Yorks' tour was immensely successful. The Duke opened the new Parliament building in Canberra with dignity and assurance and wrote to his parents: 'I have so much confidence in myself now, which I am sure comes from being able to speak properly at last'.

The birth of Princess Margaret in 1930 completed their family and the Yorks seemed set for a tranquil life in comfort, carrying out a programme of royal engagements every year. The Duke revelled in the company of his family and became a dedicated gardener. The death of George V in 1936 and the accession of his brother made Prince Albert Heir

LEFT: *Prince Albert of York, aged one.*

BELOW: *Prince Albert with his elder brother, Prince Edward, and younger sister, Princess Mary, c1900. The royal children were left largely to the care of nannies and nursemaids, seeing their parents only in the evenings. Prince Edward (later Duke of Windsor) recalled that one nanny pinched him immediately before his evening visit to his parents, 'The sobbing and bawling this treatment invariably involved understandably puzzled, worried and finally annoyed' the Duke and Duchess.*

Presumptive, but the prospect of the throne was still remote. The new king was only 18 months his senior and was still likely to marry and produce an heir.

It gradually became clear, however, that the King's preferred spouse was unacceptable to the Establishment, the country and the royal family, and on 17 November 1936 King Edward told his brother that he was determined to marry Mrs Simpson whatever the consequences. The Duke of York was struck dumb with horror, while his younger brother, the Duke of Kent fumed: 'He is besotted on that woman . . . One can't get a sensible word out of him'. The Duchess of York wrote to the King begging him to be kind to Bertie: ' . . . We want you to be happy more than anything else, but it's awfully difficult for Bertie!' Although there is no documentary evidence, it has been rumoured that consideration was given to offering the throne to the Duke of Kent, the youngest of George V's sons. The Duke of York, it was believed, would never be able to undertake all the arduous public duties of a monarch; moreover, the Duke of Kent had a son to succeed him. As the crisis was already traumatic enough, it is probably fortunate that no-one succeeded in tampering further with the succession.

After much prevarication, the King finally told the Duke of York that he would abdicate on 7 December. Two days later Bertie told Queen Mary the outcome; 'I broke down and sobbed like a child', he later wrote.

LEFT: *The Princess of Wales (later Queen Mary) with her eldest sons, 1903. George V and Queen Mary have often been accused of being indifferent parents; Lady Airlie, lady-in-waiting for nearly 50 years, believed 'The tragedy was that neither had any understanding of a child's mind'.*

BELOW: *Prince Albert with Princess Mary. The only girl in a family of five sons, Princess Mary was an excellent rider: 'My sister was a horse until she came out' wrote Prince Albert.*

He witnessed the Instrument of Abdication on 10 December and announced that he would be known as George VI, a conscious attempt at continuity with his father's reign.

The new king faced the future with trepidation; he was intimidated by the sheer amount of work and knew that in the public imagination he did not quite match up to his elder brother's glamorous image. Driven by an implacable sense of obligation, however, he went ahead with the coronation plans and was crowned on 12 May 1937 in his brother's place.

George VI could not have inherited the throne at a more difficult time in international affairs, and when it became clear that appeasement of Hitler's Germany was not working, he did all he could to improve

relations with Britain's closest allies. In the summer of 1938 the King and Queen made a triumphant state visit to France, and in May 1939 their visit to Washington jammed the streets with cheering crowds. More importantly, it gave the King a chance to gauge American feelings on the European situation and measure support for a possible war in Europe. When hostilities finally broke out in September 1939, the King and Queen worked to inspire the country, leading by example and living as far as possible in a manner similar to the majority of their subjects. The King was never seen in public in civilian clothes, a means of stressing that he was on active service. The Queen, on the other hand, deliberately never adopted any sort of uniform, always appearing elegantly dressed. A born actress, she knew that this would temporarily lift people's spirits and perhaps remind them of what they were fighting for. During one visit the Queen was given a particularly lavish meal. Eventually she turned to the mayor and said: 'You know, at Buckingham Palace we're very careful to observe the rationing regulations'. The mayor replied: 'Oh, well then, your Majesty, you'll be glad of a proper do'.

The King and Queen not only toured Britain, but the King also made several visits to his forces overseas. He developed a close relationship with his prime minister, Winston Churchill, a man of whom he had originally been suspicious in 1940, and was loath to see him leave office in 1945. The strain of the war took its toll on George VI; it aged him and affected his health irrevocably. With his family he embarked on a tour of South Africa in 1947. It meant that he missed the worst winter in Britain in living memory, but the tour itself was extremely arduous and the King lost 17 pounds in weight. He also suffered from cramp in both legs, an early sign of the arteriosclerosis which was to kill him.

For the next five years George VI found solace, as ever, in his family, but his health was deteriorating. Princess Elizabeth married Philip Mountbatten in 1947, and the arrival of his first grandchild the following year rallied the King. He had a lung removed in May 1951 and his health improved temporarily, so much so that there was a national service of thanksgiving in December. He was seen in public for the last time on 31 January as he waved farewell to his daughter and her husband at Heathrow airport. The public were shocked by his gaunt features as he stood hatless in the cold January wind. Six days later he died peacefully, but prematurely, at Sandringham, aged 56.

ABOVE AND BELOW LEFT: *Prince Albert excelled at sports. He had excellent hand-eye co-ordination and it was the one area in which he outshone his elder brother.*

BELOW AND RIGHT: *Prince Albert first met his future wife, Lady Elizabeth Bowes-Lyon, at a children's tea party in 1905. Their marriage was a great success and provided Bertie with more security than he had ever known before.*

RIGHT: *Notoriously gruff with his own sons, George V was charming to his daughters-in-law. When he died in 1935, the Duchess of York wrote 'I miss him dreadfully . . . he never spoke one unkind or abrupt word to me, and was always ready to listen and give advice on one's own silly little affairs . . .'*

LEFT, TOP RIGHT AND RIGHT: *Prince Albert, Duke of York, married Lady Elizabeth Bowes-Lyon on 26 April 1923 in Westminster Abbey; the first time a royal prince had been married there for over 500 years. The wedding was the bride's first experience of the overwhelming public interest that she dreaded, and which had nearly prevented her from marrying the Prince.*

ABOVE AND RIGHT: *The Duke and Duchess of York maintained a low-profile social life. They enjoyed country weekends and only went abroad on official business. Their first child, Princess Elizabeth, was born on 21 April 1926, 'a child to make our happiness complete', wrote the Duke.*

FACING PAGE AND BELOW LEFT: *The Duke and Duchess of York enjoyed many years of happy family life. Princess Margaret was born in 1930, and the pictures of the York family at this time contrasted with those of the Prince of Wales and his sophisticated parties. Determined to echo the idyllic childhood of the Duchess, rather than the grim experiences of the Duke, the Yorks laid less emphasis on formal education and more on fun in their daughters' upbringing.*

THESE PAGES: *The death of his father and his brother's abdication made 1936 an exceptionally stressful year for George VI, but his coronation on 12 May 1937 perhaps boosted his morale. Acutely aware of the* spiritual significance of the ceremony, he gained strength from his consecration as king. The public gave him their full support, roaring 'We want the King' late into the night outside Buckingham Palace.*

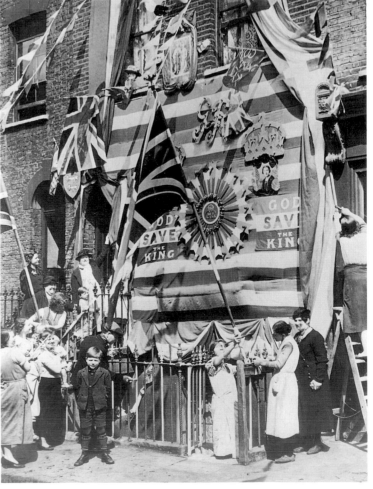

ABOVE: *Many of George VI's official duties as king were little different from those he had carried out as Duke of York. During the war he was assiduous about troop inspections; here he reviews American soldiers training in Northern Ireland in 1942.*

RIGHT: *The royal family make their state entry into Edinburgh by train, 1937.*

ABOVE: *King George VI and Queen Elizabeth participate in the annual Ceremony of the Order of the Garter, 1937.*

CENTRE LEFT AND BELOW LEFT: *At the time of the abdication, there were many who wondered whether the Duke of York would be strong enough for the onerous job of monarch. He was afflicted with a stammer, and often seemed nervous in public, but he seemed to blossom in the early years of his reign, becoming more confident and gaining strength from the support of the public and his ministers.*

THIS PAGE: *The political situation in Europe had rarely been more fraught than in 1939. The King and Queen made three state visits before the outbreak of hostilities, to France, the United States and Canada, all of which were designed to cement diplomatic relations. Links with Roosevelt's America were particularly important, and the royal couple made an excellent impression on everyone, from the President down. He described them as 'very delightful and understanding people who knew a great deal not only about foreign affairs in general but also about social legislation'.*

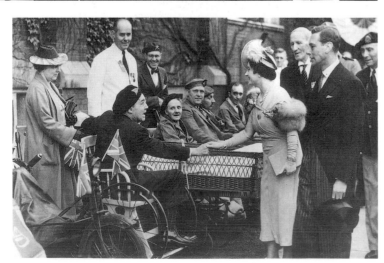

THIS PAGE: *Britain's prime minister on the outbreak of World War II was Neville Chamberlain (top), a man whom George VI admired, but who was distrusted by many of his party as an appeaser of Hitler. Forced to resign in June 1940, he was succeeded by Winston Churchill (right). The relationship between King and* *prime minister was initially wary, not least because Churchill had been vocal in his support of Edward VIII in 1936. In 1940, however, it quickly became clear that Churchill's qualities as a war leader were outstanding, and the King realized Britain could have no better prime minister in time of national crisis.*

THIS PAGE: *With the bombing of mainland Britain, the King and Queen became symbols of British resistance to the Nazis. Both refused all suggestions that they or the princesses should be evacuated to Canada. The King began practising rifle shooting in the gardens of Buckingham Palace, and the Queen had daily lessons in firing a revolver. The royal couple's visits to bomb sites around the country had a very positive effect on public morale, simply because their concern was so genuine. When Buckingham Palace was bombed on 13 Sepember 1940 (left), the Queen said 'I'm glad we have been bombed; I feel I can look the East End in the face'.*

ABOVE: *In October 1944 the King spent six days with the newly-promoted Field Marshal Montgomery at Eindhoven. They both enjoyed the visit, Monty writing that the King 'stayed with me as an ordinary soldier guest with no formality at all'.*

LEFT: *The royal family suffered their own casualty in August 1942, when the King's youngest brother, Prince George, Duke of Kent, was killed in a plane crash in Scotland. After a wild youth, Prince George had married Princess Marina of Greece in 1934, and revelled in family life with their three children, Prince Edward, Princess Alexandra, and Prince Michael, who had only been christened three weeks before his father's death.*

ABOVE: *The royal family wave to crowds celebrating VJ Day – victory over Japan – and the final end to war, 24 August 1945.*

LEFT: *President Truman was received by George VI shortly afer the Potsdam Conference, August 1945.*

BELOW: *The princesses broadcast to the children of the Empire, 1940.*

ABOVE RIGHT: *The royal family at Sandringham, 1943.*

RIGHT: *Ascot, 1949. The strain of the war years did untold damage to George VI's health.*

ABOVE AND LEFT: *George VI's family was central to his life, and visitors to the various royal homes often remarked on the happy atmosphere. Field Marshal Alan Brooke noted that 'the King and Queen and their two daughters provide one of the very best examples of English family life. A thorough close-knit and happy family all wrapped up in each other . . .'*

ABOVE AND LEFT: *The King adored his daughters, and with Princess Elizabeth's marriage in 1947 came the family break-up he had always dreaded. After initial reservations, he came to like and respect Prince Philip, and enjoyed the company of his grandchildren, Prince Charles and Princess Anne.*

OVERLEAF: *George VI died on 6 February 1952 after a long struggle with cancer. Churchill broadcast his obituary the following day: 'During those months the King walked with death . . . We all saw him approach his journey's end'.*

CHAPTER FIVE

THE QUEEN MOTHER

The woman who twice declined a prince's proposal of marriage and was reluctant to marry into the royal family because she felt she would 'never again be free to think, speak or act as I really feel', has emerged as one of the most popular royals this century. To onlookers, it may seem as though Queen Elizabeth, the Queen Mother, has led a charmed life. She married the King's second son at the age of 23, had two pretty daughters and, a decade or so later, slipped effortlessly into the rôle of queen. After the death of her husband she became, almost overnight, the nation's favourite grandmother. It reads like a fairytale, but few people realize that Queen Elizabeth has faced many crises in her life and has overcome them all by sheer strength of character. Part of her success is perhaps due to her ability to view the royal rôle in a detached manner unavailable to those born to the job.

Fiercely protective of her husband, she apparently believes that his life was shortened by the stresses of the war, and was never able to forgive her brother-in-law and Mrs Simpson who thrust the throne upon George VI. The abdication of Edward VIII dramatically changed the life of her family, and the new queen dealt with this crisis in a characteristically practical manner. She ensured that her elder daughter learnt about constitutional history and provided her husband with an understanding and totally supportive partner. The Queen's sister commented on the royal marriage: 'They were so particularly together. The King was a rock to her, indeed to all of us. In fundamental things she leant on him'.

The public trials of the war years were succeeded by a far more personal anguish. The King, worn out by the strain of the war, was suffering from arteriosclerosis. He became subject to depression and from 1948 was in a great deal of pain. When lung cancer was diagnosed in September 1951, the Queen kept the true seriousness of the condition from her husband. The fortitude with which she coped with his

illness and early death was quite remarkable, but there is no doubt about the extent of her bereavement.

Widowed at the comparatively early age of 51, she retreated from the public eye in the months following the King's death. By the summer of 1953 she seemed to have picked up the threads of her life once more, devoting herself to her family, horse racing, and the renovation of her new Scottish home, the Castle of Mey. She adored her grandchildren and it was evident that both her daughters relied on her advice. Princess Margaret, in particular, needed her mother's guidance during the 1950s. She had fallen in love with one of her father's equerries, Group Captain Peter Townsend, a divorced man 16 years her senior. With the shadow of the abdication never far away, the Queen Mother was desperately worried about the effect of such a marriage on the country, but at the same time was completely sympathetic to her daughter's plight.

The Queen Mother resumed official duties in 1953, embarking on extensive foreign tours to Rhodesia, Canada and the USA. She continued to enjoy foreign travel until well into her eighties and has kept up a punishing round of public engagements, working at a pace that would exhaust lesser mortals. It is this devotion to duty, combined with a great natural charm, that has endeared her to people the world over. In 1980 there was a national service of thanksgiving for her eightieth birthday. The Archbishop of Canterbury seemed to sum up the Queen Mother's remarkable contribution to the nation in his address. 'Royalty,' he said, 'puts a human face on the operations of government', and for over 50 years the Queen Mother has done just that. A large part of the public respect for the monarchy stems from the Queen Mother's tireless, dignified work.

RIGHT: *Queen Elizabeth in 1951.*

THESE PAGES: *Lady Elizabeth Bowes-Lyon was born in 1900 at Glamis Castle, the youngest daughter of the Earl of Strathmore. 'I have nothing but wonderfully happy memories of childhood days at home' she wrote many years later. She grew into a confident, charming and beautiful young woman, who came to be surrounded by a string of admirers when she was a debutante, among whom was George V's shy and diffident second son, Prince Albert, Duke of York. He was completely captivated by her, but their romance was blighted by Elizabeth's reluctance to surrender her freedom. When their engagement was eventually announced in January 1923, Chips Channon noted that Prince Albert 'is the luckiest of men . . . there's not a man in England today that doesn't envy him. The clubs are in gloom'.*

THIS PAGE: *The wedding of the Duke and Duchess of York in April 1923 (left) was followed three years later by the birth of their elder daughter, Princess Elizabeth (below). In January 1927 the Duke and Duchess left their baby in the care of her grandparents for a six-month tour of Australia and New Zealand (above).*

THIS PAGE: *During the 1920s, the Duchess of York injected an element of glamour into the royal family. Her love and support for Prince Albert gave him new confidence in carrying out his official duties, and the Duchess herself charmed people wherever she went.*

LEFT: *Queen Elizabeth ensured that her daughters grew up in a secure and loving family atmosphere; she and the King saw a great deal more of their children than many other upper-class parents.*

ABOVE, LEFT AND RIGHT: *The Duchess of York evolved her own characteristic style of dress. She had an unfashionably curvaceous figure, but with the help of dress designers like Norman Hartnell, acquired a classically elegant image.*

ABOVE: *The royal family at the coronation of George VI and Queen Elizabeth. From left: Princess Mary, the Princess Royal; the Duchess of Gloucester; the Duke of Gloucester; Queen Mary; the King; Princess Margaret; Princess Elizabeth; the Queen; the Duke of Kent; the Duchess of Kent; Queen Maud of Norway (the only surviving sister of George V).*

RIGHT: *Queen Elizabeth with Eleanor Roosevelt during the state visit to the United States, 1939.*

RIGHT AND BELOW: *In February 1947 the royal family embarked on HMS Vanguard for an imperial tour of South Africa. For two months they toured the country on the 'White Train', an experience they found both exhilarating and exhausting. Princess Elizabeth remarked that 'Mummy and Pop' were just about done in, but that she and Margaret were enjoying every moment of it.*

ABOVE: *Cecil Beaton's 1949 portrait of Queen Elizabeth.*

RIGHT AND BELOW: *In the months immediately following the death of her husband in 1952, Queen Elizabeth retreated from public life. By the autumn of 1953 she felt able to resume official duties, often accompanied by Princess Margaret. Her younger daughter needed her mother's support at this time, having fallen in love with one of her father's equerries, Group Captain Peter Townsend, a divorced man 16 years her senior. The couple wanted to marry, but Parliament regarded a royal marriage to a divorcé as anathema, and in 1955 Princess Margaret publicly declared that 'mindful of the Church's teaching that Christian marriage is indissoluble', she would not marry Townsend.*

RIGHT: *The Queen Mother, followed by the Duke and Duchess of Gloucester, visiting Oundle School, 1956.*

OPPOSITE PAGE: *The Queen with her daughters during World War II.*

ABOVE: *The Queen Mother's interest in racing dates from 1949, when she purchased a steeplechaser called Monaveen. Initially a distraction from the King's illness, horse racing became a passion.*

RIGHT: *An accomplished pianist, Queen Elizabeth's skills have been inherited by Princess Margaret.*

RIGHT: *Queen Elizabeth became Chancellor of London University in 1955 and for 25 years showed a very real interest in, and concern for, student affairs. She is seen here dancing an eightsome reel at the Senate House Ball in 1958.*

BELOW: *An energetic traveller, Queen Elizabeth has always enjoyed foreign tours. In 1954 she visited Canada and the United States where she was guest of honour at Columbia University's Charter Day.*

RIGHT: *The Queen Mother celebrated her eightieth birthday in 1980. She is pictured here surrounded by her grandchildren. Standing, from left, Viscount Linley, Prince Andrew, Prince Charles and Prince Edward; seated, Lady Sarah Armstrong-Jones and Princess Anne.*

ABOVE LEFT AND RIGHT, AND
LEFT: *Photographs taken at the
Badminton Horse Trials
showing the Queen Mother
combining her two great loves:
watching equestrian displays
surrounded by her family and
friends.*

RIGHT: *Queen Elizabeth listens to recordings about the D-Day landings as she is shown the Overlord Embroidery, 1978. She is patron of many charities, a number of them associated with World War II, and continues to carry out a full schedule of official duties. In 1990, when she was 90, she had 122 public engagements.*

ABOVE AND RIGHT: *The Queen Mother has a close relationship with all her grandchildren; she has always enjoyed their company, and they still seek her advice today. She is seen above with the 10-year-old Prince Andrew in 1970, and right, with Princess Margaret's children Lady Sarah Armstrong-Jones and David, Viscount Linley in 1971.*

ABOVE AND BELOW: *Queen Elizabeth has charmed people throughout her life with her ready smile and gentle wit.*

LEFT: *With Princess Margaret during a state carriage procession.*

LEFT: *Four generations. The Queen Mother holds the infant Prince William, and shares a joke with Prince Charles and the Queen, 1982.*

OPPOSITE PAGE: *Queen Elizabeth leaves the Garter Ceremony with the Prince of Wales. They are very close, and she played a major part in encouraging his romance with Lady Diana Spencer.*

CHAPTER SIX

ELIZABETH II
1952-

After 40 years on the throne as Queen of the United Kingdom and Head of the Commonwealth, Queen Elizabeth II is one of the world's most experienced heads of state. Born in 1926, the elder daughter of George V's second son, the prospect of the young Princess Elizabeth of York inheriting the throne was remote. Not only did the world expect her father's elder brother, the Prince of Wales, to marry, but the young princess' place in the line of succession could have been altered by the birth of a young brother. The abdication of her uncle, Edward VIII, in December 1936 changed her life irrevocably, and Princess Elizabeth and her younger sister Princess Margaret were immediately aware of their different destinies. When Elizabeth told her sister that their father was King, Margaret asked: 'Does that mean that you will have to be the next queen?' 'Yes, some day', her sister replied. 'Poor you', said Margaret.

As children, Princess Elizabeth and Princess Margaret were brought up together and treated equally by their family. Often dressed identically, they were known to the public as 'the little princesses' and it was not really until the end of the war, when Princess Elizabeth was 18, that they developed separate public identities. In private, courtiers and relations noticed how different the girls were: Princess Elizabeth (Lilibet to her family) was the serious older sister, Margaret more frivolous and fun-loving. They were brought up almost completely apart from other children and were educated by private tutors. It was not until she was 18 that Princess Elizabeth had a little more contact with the outside world, when she insisted on serving in the armed forces like other people her age. She joined the women's branch of the Army, the ATS (Auxiliary Territorial Service) and learnt mechanics at Camberley, emerging a month before the end of the war as Second Subaltern Windsor. Queen Elizabeth II is the only British monarch to be a qualified motor mechanic.

The matter of the Princess' marriage was a delicate one, and an area of potential conflict, if only for the reason that George VI was reluctant to admit that his daughter was old enough for romance. The princesses came into contact with very few young men, and although her parents attempted to widen her social circle in the 1940s, Elizabeth fell in love with one of her cousins. Princess Elizabeth married Lieutenant Philip Mountbatten on 14 November 1947. His humble title disguised a lineage almost as exalted as that of his wife. A prince of the beleaguered Greek royal family, Philip was not only a nephew of Lord Mountbatten but also a great-grandson of Queen Victoria. He had been educated in Britain and distinguished himself in the Royal Navy during World War II. Despite his background, however, he was not considered entirely suitable as a prospective husband for the heir to the British throne. George V's biographer, Harold Nicolson, believed that the royal family felt that Philip was 'rough, ill-mannered, uneducated and would probably not be faithful . . . ' He was certainly very different from the aristocratic army officers with whom the princesses usually mixed. It seems safe to say that, after 45 years of marriage, the Duke of Edinburgh has confounded his early critics. He adapted to the rôle of royal consort gradually, evidently finding it irksome in the early days. The traditional Palace protocol infuriated him, and he has done much to remove some of the 'red tape' that plagues the lives of the royal family. Obliged to take second place in public, in private Prince Philip is very much the head of the family.

The premature death of George VI in February 1952 destroyed any ambitions the young Duke and Duchess of Edinburgh may have had for a quiet family life. Having dedicated herself to the service of her country on her 21st birthday, the new Queen embarked on the business of sovereignty at the age of 25. Her coronation in June 1953 captured the imagination of the

RIGHT: *Queen Elizabeth II with her corgis in Scotland, 1972.*

nation and provoked many comments about a new 'Elizabethan age'.

The new queen had been trained in the basic duties of a monarch by her father. She had studied constitutional history with the Provost of Eton and appeared to have no trouble in grasping the complex political briefings she received from her ministers. Her first prime minister was the 78-year-old Winston Churchill, who grew exceptionally fond of his new sovereign, and often emerged from his weekly audience saying 'What a very attractive and intelligent young woman'. Queen Elizabeth has seen nine prime ministers come and go, all of whom attest to her astuteness and faultless political skill. 'I shall certainly advise my successor to do his homework before his audience and to read all his telegrams and Cabinet Committee papers in time', said Harold Wilson on his retirement in 1976, 'or he will feel like an unprepared schoolboy'. The Queen has no respite from the red boxes of state papers which require her signature. They follow her everywhere, and she was even to be found reading some in bed a few hours after the birth of Prince Andrew in 1960.

The Queen has presided over Britain during 40 years of great change. The country's global rôle has altered considerably since she became queen; Britain is no longer the world power that it once was, but her sovereign presides over the Commonwealth, an

LEFT: *Princess Elizabeth of York with her parents in 1927.*

BELOW AND RIGHT: *Known as 'Lilibet' to her family, Princess Elizabeth enjoyed a charmed childhood, shielded by her parents from the public gaze as far as possible.*

LEFT: *The 10-year-old Princess Elizabeth arrives with her mother and sister at a wedding in 1936.*

international forum which brings together the heads of government of between a quarter and a third of the world's population. One by one, Britain's former colonies have become independent, although many have retained their links through the Commonwealth, an institution which has been described as the most civilized way of disbanding the Empire.

The monarchy itself has come in for a considerable amount of criticism during Elizabeth II's reign. The pre-war deference accorded to the royal family by the press has been gradually eroded, beginning in 1957 when John Grigg (then Lord Altrincham) criticized the royal entourage as 'a tight little enclave of British ladies and gentlemen', which did not reflect the much wider composition of Britain and the Commonwealth, and the Queen's manner of public speaking. Whether or not provoked by Altrincham, the Queen did make

some radical changes at the end of the 1950s. The presentation of debutantes at Court was abolished in 1958; the Queen consulted a voice coach before her next Christmas broadcast; and both the number and the scope of royal garden parties was broadened.

It was not until 1969 that the royal family really embraced the media, however, with the BBC film, *Royal Family*. Allowed unprecedented access to the royal family (although occasionally dogged by Prince Philip's shouts of 'Don't bring your bloody cameras so close to the Queen'), the public saw the private family behind the public facade – relaxing, barbecuing, cracking jokes. This new openness certainly helped to bring the monarchy closer to the people, but it was the beginning of a dangerous new trend. Having seen the world's richest woman and her family behaving like everyone else, the public have demanded more. Not content with official portraits and the occasional documentary, they now expect constant access to the royal family, a demand that the popular press tries to fulfil. The mystique of the monarchy is gradually disappearing, and new claims are made on it, such as subjecting the Queen to taxation. Instead of hiding from problems behind the facade of official Buckingham Palace press releases, the monarchy must develop a strategy for change in order to meet the challenges of the twenty-first century.

The wider publicity accorded to the House of Windsor has probably affected the Queen's children more seriously than the rest of the family. The Queen and Prince Philip tried to provide a more normal childhood than the cloistered upbringing experienced by the Queen and Princess Margaret. They wanted them to have more contact with the outside world, so the Princes Charles, Andrew and Edward all attended Gordonstoun School in Scotland, and Princess Anne

LEFT: *Princess Elizabeth and Princess Margaret in costume during a wartime production of* Cinderella *at Windsor Castle, 1941.*

TOP: *A formal portrait of Princess Elizabeth in Girl Guide uniform, 1944.*

ABOVE: *Princess Elizabeth with Queen Mary on her eighteenth birthday in 1944. Queen Mary's influence on her granddaughter was paramount, instilling a firm sense of duty in the young Princess.*

RIGHT: *The royal family visit Dartmouth Naval College, 1939. Just visible second right is Prince Philip of Greece whom Princess Elizabeth met for the first time on this occasion.*

BELOW, LEFT AND RIGHT: *The young princesses, Elizabeth and Margaret (right) spent the war years in comparative seclusion at Windsor Castle, the royal palace that the Queen still regards as 'home' today.*

was educated at Benenden in Kent. It is as young adults that the royal children have had most problems. An equestrian of Olympic standard, Princess Anne's every fall was recorded by the press; Prince Andrew was tailed by newsmen with zoom lenses when on holiday after service in the Falklands Campaign; Prince Edward's decision to leave the Marines was made all the more difficult by the public interest in him; and Prince Charles was barely able to talk to a young woman during the 1970s without the tabloid press hinting at his imminent marriage. Princess Anne

probably summed up the feelings of them all: 'I don't do stunts. I don't go for them anyway. Why should I do it to please their [newspaper] editors?'

The demands of the job are relentless. The Queen herself has accepted her fate philosophically, commenting that she rather likes having a job for life – so few people do these days. She has made it clear many times that abdication is not an option; the Queen Mother has said that the Queen appreciates the 'spiritual quality of the commitment made at the coronation . . . to serve and to reign . . .' The Queen may be a constitutional monarch and be therefore barred from imposing her wishes on the government, but she can express her views with vigour. 'You can't cancel Concorde', she told the hapless Minister of Technology who suggested ending the Anglo-French partnership because of a lack of customers.

It has been said that one can set one's watch by the monarch's timetable: Christmas at Sandringham, spring at Buckingham Palace, Easter at Windsor, the summer season in London, a stint at Holyrood House in Edinburgh, before two months at Balmoral from August to October, when she moves back to London. Much of the royal ceremonial has remained unchanged for most of this century, and under Elizabeth II the monarchy has retained much of its grandeur and formality. The Queen brings an iron self-control to her job. She rarely shows her emotions, perhaps the only time being in 1966 when she visited the site of the Aberfan mining disaster. Her public facade hides a woman of great warmth and humour, but she feels that the dignity of her position requires a little distance and restraint – and the majority of her reserved British subjects would probably agree with her.

King Farouk of Egypt prophesied that by the end of the century there would only be five royal houses left: hearts, spades, diamonds, clubs and the House of Windsor. The survival of the House of Windsor is due in no small part to Elizabeth II's devotion to duty; she has strengthened the monarchy through her own strength as an individual.

ABOVE: *Princess Elizabeth persuaded her father to let her join one of the armed services in 1945. She had barely finished a course in vehicle maintenance before the war ended, but she obviously enjoyed the whole experience, her mother remarking wryly that 'we've had sparking plugs throughout dinner every night this week'.*

BELOW: *Princess Elizabeth and Princess Margaret at Buckingham Palace in 1946.*

RIGHT AND CENTRE RIGHT:
The son of Prince Andrew of Greece, Prince Philip had a peripatetic childhood after the Greek royal family lost its throne in 1922. His parents lived apart and he was educated in France (right) and in Britain at Gordonstoun (centre right).

LEFT AND ABOVE: *A great-granddaughter of Queen Victoria, Prince Philip's mother (left) founded an order of Greek Orthodox nuns. Her brother, Lord Mountbatten (above), was broadly responsible for Philip's upbringing, encouraging him in his naval career, and in his relationship with Princess Elizabeth.*

THESE PAGES: *Princess
Elizabeth first met Prince Philip
in 1939 on a visit to Dartmouth
Naval College when she was 13
and he was 18. They began to
correspond during the war, and
Philip spent some of his leave
from the Navy at Windsor,
where their friendship deepened.
Despite the fact that Philip
came from an impoverished
branch of the exiled Greek royal
family, he and Elizabeth were
third cousins, so no-one could
really object to his background.
A discreet picture of him
allegedly appeared beside the
Princess' bed during the war,
but it was not until 1946 that,
in the Prince's words, 'we
began to think about it
[marriage] seriously, and even
talk about it'. Their engagement
was announced on 10 July 1947,
Philip having renounced his
Greek titles and become plain
Lieutenant Philip Mountbatten,
RN. On their wedding day, 20
November 1947, the King
conferred on Philip the title of
Duke of Edinburgh.*

RIGHT: *The wedding of Princess Elizabeth and the Duke of Edinburgh provided the first post-war opportunity for a reunion of the surviving crowned heads of Europe. After six years of wartime austerity, the wedding seemed to the nation almost like a fairy-tale, and gifts and food parcels poured in from around Britain and the Empire. Buckingham Palace had emphasized that the Princess had, like other brides, received an extra ration of clothing coupons to help with her trousseau; unlike most of them, however, she had also been given vast amounts of stunning material by the public, enabling Norman Hartnell to create a spectacular wedding dress. As Queen Mary's lady-in-waiting, Lady Airlie, recalled, 'Most of us were sadly shabby – anyone fortunate enough to have a new dress drew all eyes – but all the famous diamonds came out again, even though most of them had not been cleaned since 1939'.*

OPPOSITE PAGE: *The Duke and Duchess of Edinburgh spent their honeymoon at Broadlands, Lord Mountbatten's home, and then travelled on to Malta.*

ABOVE: *The royal family in 1947. The King felt his daughter's loss very keenly, writing to her a few days after her wedding: 'Your leaving us has left a great blank in our lives, but do remember that your old home is still yours and do come back to it as much and as often as possible. I can see that you are sublimely happy with Philip, which is right, but don't forget us . . .'*

LEFT: *Princess Elizabeth and Prince Philip at a barn dance in Canada, 1951.*

THESE PAGES: *With the birth of Prince Charles in 1948, and of Princess Anne in 1950, Princess Elizabeth expected to be able to spend several years enjoying her young family while the Duke of Edinburgh pursued his naval career. Prince Philip was posted to Malta in 1949, and until 1951 Princess Elizabeth shuttled between the life of a naval wife in Malta and the duties of a princess in London. These halcyon days came to an end with the death of George VI in February 1952.*

RIGHT AND BELOW: *There was much debate in 1953 about exposing the ritual and mystique of a coronation to the full glare of television. In the face of opposition from the Archbishop of Canterbury, the prime minister and the Cabinet, the Queen insisted that as many of her subjects as possible should be able to see the ceremony. The BBC provided seven-and-a-half hours of coverage, which was hailed as a landmark in broadcasting history, and was watched by 20 million people in Britain alone.*

ABOVE: *The accession of Queen Elizabeth II is proclaimed at Charing Cross on 8 February 1952, the day after the Queen herself arrived back from Kenya where she had received the news of her father's death.*

RIGHT: *The population of Britain and the Commonwealth was approximately 650 million in 1953, and by 2 June 1953, the day of the coronation, London was full of patriotic subjects determined to celebrate the historic occasion.*

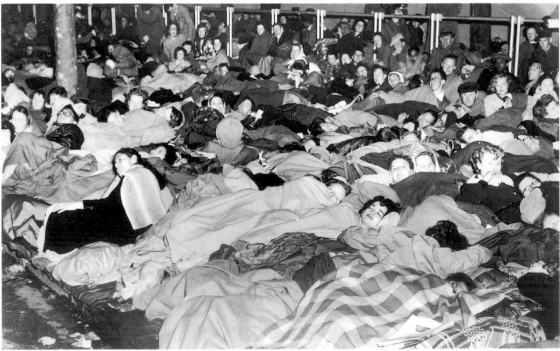

LEFT AND RIGHT: *There was a 16-month gap between the accession of Elizabeth II in 1952 and her coronation the following year. This was due to simple logistical matters, such as organization, Court mourning for the late King, and the preference for staging the procession in the summer (although in the event the weather was showery and grey). Prince Philip played a key role in the organization, and the Queen and her advisers spent long weeks rehearsing the ceremony.*

BELOW: *A coronation portrait of the immediate royal family. Back row, from left: the Dukes of Gloucester, Edinburgh and Kent; front row, from left: Princess Alexandra of Kent; Prince Michael of Kent; Princess Marina, Duchess of Kent; Princess Margaret; the Queen; Queen Elizabeth, the Queen Mother; Princess Mary, the Princess Royal; Princess Alice, Duchess of Gloucester; Prince William of Gloucester and Prince Richard of Gloucester.*

ABOVE: *The Queen and her family watch an RAF fly-past from the balcony at Buckingham Palace after the coronation ceremony.*

LEFT: *Watched by Clement Attlee, the Queen shakes hands with her first prime minister, Winston Churchill.*

RIGHT: *The first Commonwealth Economic Summit of Elizabeth II's reign, May 1952. Described as the most civilized way of dismantling the Empire, the British Commonwealth now brings together the heads of government of between a quarter and a third of the world's population.*

RIGHT AND BELOW: *A man of forthright opinions, the Duke of Edinburgh has established a clearly-defined public persona, but in the early years he found the constraints of royal life irksome. Destined to take second place to his wife on public occasions, such as the state opening of Parliament (below), in private he is very much head of the family.*

LEFT: *An official portrait of the Queen and the Duke of Edinburgh, released to coincide with their state visit to Canada and the USA in 1957.*

ABOVE: *The Queen broadcast her first televised Christmas message to the Commonwealth in 1957. She recalled, 'The first time my white skin and broad jaw made my face come out like a huge white plate with dark cavities containing black boot buttons; my hair was parted in the centre and [it] looked like a white line down a main road. It had to be blacked and yellow paint daubed on my cheeks and the tip of my nose'.*

THIS PAGE: *The Queen and Prince Philip embarked on a number of foreign tours during the first 10 years of her reign, visiting a large part of the Commonwealth, from New Zealand in 1954 (left), to Nigeria in 1957 (right) and India in 1961 (above).*

THIS PAGE: *A more frivolous and fun-loving character than her sister, Princess Margaret wished to marry one of her father's equerries, Group Captain Peter Townsend (standing below) in 1953. Ironically, her father had encouraged their friendship, regarding Townsend as a steadying influence on the young Princess. The one drawback to their plans for marriage was Townsend's divorce; the royal family approved of him and liked him, but with the shadow of the abdication hanging over them, could not accept him as a suitor unless Margaret renounced her claim to the throne. Forty years on, her niece, Princess Anne, is not only divorced from her first husband, but has married another former equerry, Commander Timothy Laurence.*

THESE PAGES: *In 1960 Princess Margaret announced her engagement to Anthony Armstrong-Jones, a young photographer who had been commissioned to produce portraits of Prince Charles and Princess Anne a couple of years earlier. Sharing a love of the arts, they were married in 1960, and the Queen ennobled her brother-in-law as the Earl of Snowdon. Early in their marriage Snowdon joined his wife on public engagements and foreign tours, but he also continued with his photographic career, remarking several years later, 'I am not a member of the royal family; I am married to a member of the royal family'.*

THIS PAGE: *The births of Prince Andrew in 1960 (left) and Prince Edward in 1964 (right) completed the Queen's 'second' family. More comfortable with her rôle as monarch by the second decade of her reign, the Queen was able to spend more time with her younger sons than she had with her elder children.*

OPPOSITE PAGE: *Foreign tours undertaken by the royal family are subject to meticulous planning. The tours are preceded by visits from security officers, press secretaries and other officials who ensure that events will run smoothly, and that exotic methods of transport such as those pictured here are completely safe.*

LEFT: *'I think everyone will concede that today, of all occasions, I should begin my speech with "My Husband and I"' . . . In 1972 the Queen and Prince Philip celebrated their Silver Wedding with a service in Westminster Abbey, followed by lunch at the Guildhall.*

ABOVE: *A portrait of the royal family taken in 1972 for the Silver Wedding.*

RIGHT: *The Queen with her oldest and youngest sons, Prince Charles and Prince Edward, at Windsor during the late 1960s.*

LEFT: *Princess Anne was a competitor in the British equestrian team at the Montreal Olympics in 1976 and, like many others, was joined by the rest of her family.*

LEFT, ABOVE AND CENTRE: *The Silver Jubilee in 1977 encouraged a national outpouring of patriotic fervour unlike anything seen since the coronation.*

ABOVE: *The Queen opens the Bahamian Parliament, 1973. Elizabeth II is not only Queen of Great Britain, but also of 17 of the 50 countries in the Commonwealth.*

RIGHT: *The royal yacht* Britannia *provides the royal family with a base on foreign tours abroad. It is maintained at the taxpayers' expense from the Civil List allowance, and is invaluable both as an office and as a venue for returning hospitality while abroad. It was also converted for use as a hospital ship during the Falklands conflict.*

OPPOSITE PAGE: *The Queen and the Duke of Edinburgh at Balmoral.*

LEFT: *It is simple courtesy on foreign visits to adhere to local customs. An audience with the Pope in 1980 was not only remarkable as the first meeting between the head of the Church of England and the Pontiff, but also because the Queen wore the long black dress and mantilla.*

RIGHT: *In 1979 the Queen toured the Persian Gulf and is seen here with the Emir of Kuwait.*

BELOW RIGHT: *President Ronald Reagan toasts the Queen during her visit to California in 1983. It took place during some of the worst storms in living memory, prompting Princess Margaret to ask her sister whether she had anything else to wear other than 'that horrible old mackintosh'.*

BELOW: *The Queen hosts a mini-Commonwealth Summit dinner at Buckingham Palace, 1986.*

OPPOSITE PAGE: *The Queen is a countrywoman at heart and relishes the time she is able to spend relaxing at horse trials or at the races. She never takes holidays abroad, retiring instead to Balmoral every summer.*

RIGHT AND BELOW: *Queen Elizabeth's love of horses is well known. She is an accomplished rider, as is her daughter, Princess Anne. The Queen has become an expert on bloodstock, and owns a profitable racing stable. She visits Kentucky every year for the annual sales and follows the fortunes of her horses very closely. 'If it were not for my Archbishop of Canterbury', she once said, 'I should be off in my plane to Longchamps every Sunday'.*

ABOVE: *In 1986 the Queen and the Duke of Edinburgh visited China for the first time. Seen here inspecting a guard of honour in Peking, they went to several of China's greatest monuments and were received with great warmth.*

RIGHT: *Britain has enjoyed a warm diplomatic relationship with Nepal for well over a century. The Queen and Prince Philip paid a state visit there in 1986.*

THIS PAGE: *Ascot and Derby Day at Epsom are two of the fixtures in the royal calendar. The Queen stays at Windsor for Ascot week, sometimes entertaining guests, and visits the races several times. Given the royal family's love of horses, these public engagements are probably amongst their favourites.*

ABOVE: *The Queen and Prince Philip acknowledge the crowds at Ascot.*

LEFT: *The Queen and fellow race-goers Prince and Princess Michael of Kent celebrate a win.*

BELOW: *Derby Day, and the serious nature of the day's business is reflected in the faces of the Queen and Queen Mother.*

LEFT AND RIGHT: *The annual ceremony of Trooping the Colour is Britain's biggest military parade, and is held to celebrate the sovereign's official birthday. Although of limited military significance today, it emphasizes the close links between the monarch and the armed forces. For many years the Queen rode her horse Burmese, but since he was retired in the mid-1980s, she has reviewed her troops from an open carriage.*

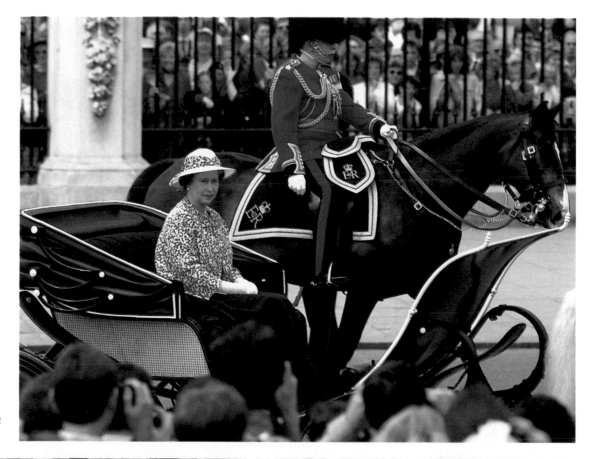

BELOW: *The ceremony for the Knights of the Garter, Britain's oldest and most exclusive order of chivalry, is held every year in St George's Chapel, Windsor.*

187

ABOVE: *The Duke of Edinburgh returns the salute at the Gulf War Parade in the City of London, 1991.*

LEFT: *Prince Charles kisses his mother's hand as he receives a polo trophy from her.*

RIGHT: *The Queen and the Duke of Edinburgh arrive for the annual state opening of Parliament. It is a ceremony rich in traditions which underline what a constitutional monarchy is all about: the monarch receives a 'Humble Address' from MPs, before reading her 'Gracious Speech', which is prepared by the government of the day, not the Palace or, indeed, the sovereign herself.*

CHAPTER SEVEN
HEIR APPARENT

Not only does the succession of the House of Windsor appear secure well into the twenty-first century, but the man who will probably be the next king of Great Britain is better prepared for the job than any of his predecessors.

Born on 14 November 1948, Prince Charles Philip Arthur George has spent his life in the public eye. His parents did their utmost to shield him from the prying eyes of journalists when he was a child, and were largely successful until he reached early adulthood. Public interest in Prince Charles has been increased by the fact that he has broken many royal barriers. He was the first heir to the throne to attend public school and to obtain a university degree, the first to train as a commando and frogman, and to pilot helicopters and supersonic jets. His education, to the credit of the Prince and his parents, has been more broadly based than that of any of his predecessors.

The Prince's education was the subject of lengthy discussion between the Queen and the Duke of Edinburgh and their advisers. Prince Philip was keen that his son should experience the discipline and stimulation of a normal school, and his eldest son duly attended his old schools, Cheam Preparatory and Gordonstoun. It was while he was at Cheam, in 1958, that the Queen declared that she was creating Charles Prince of Wales. The Prince has said that he became aware of his destiny gradually: 'I didn't wake up in my pram and say "Yippee" . . . you know. But I think it just dawns on you slowly, that people are interested in one . . .' The Prince spent six months in Australia when he was 17 and developed a life-long affection for the country and the people, partly because he found the unstuffy Australian approach to life a refreshing change: 'You are judged there on how people see you and feel about you. There are no assumptions there'.

After Gordonstoun Prince Charles went to Cambridge, and also spent a term at the University of Aberystwyth prior to his investiture as Prince of Wales in July 1969. Once he had graduated he followed royal tradition and embarked on a naval career. He also served with the RAF and with the Fleet Air Arm. He was given his own command, of the minesweeper HMS *Bronington* in 1976, but retired from active naval service later in the year to devote more time to his official duties.

'I don't really know what my rôle in life is. At the moment, I don't have one. But somehow I must find one for myself.' The Prince of Wales has spent the years since leaving the Navy in 1976 trying to do just that. He has worked hard to establish his credentials and to prepare himself for the rôle he was born to as king of England. Until he inherits the throne there is no clearly-defined job for him, but the Prince has done his utmost to find a niche for himself. To fulfil the rather nebulous rôle of heir to the throne, Prince Charles has to obey the dictates of tradition while trying to reconcile the often conflicting demands of public, Palace and Parliament – and also those of the private Prince himself.

His life can perhaps be divided into three compartments: ceremonial, public/everyday duties, and his private interests. Ceremonial duties include Trooping the Colour, the Garter Ceremony, state visits abroad, and deputizing for the Queen at investitures or as a Councillor of State. In addition to the usual round of official visits and speeches, the Prince's public duties include his work for the Prince's Trust, the charity he established in 1976 to support young people. As Duke of Cornwall, he takes an active interest in duchy administration and farming methods, putting into practice some of his well-known beliefs about environmentally-friendly techniques. The Duchy of Cornwall owns some 130,000 acres of land around the country, including 44 acres in London, and the

RIGHT: *The polo-playing Prince, 1988.*

190

LEFT: *Queen Mary holding the infant Prince Charles in 1948.*

RIGHT: *Both Prince Charles and Princess Anne were born before their mother succeeded to the throne. In 1951 the family was living at Clarence House in London.*

BELOW RIGHT: *Corgis are a permanent fixture in the lives of the royal family. Here the six-year-old Prince Charles plays with Honey at Windsor.*

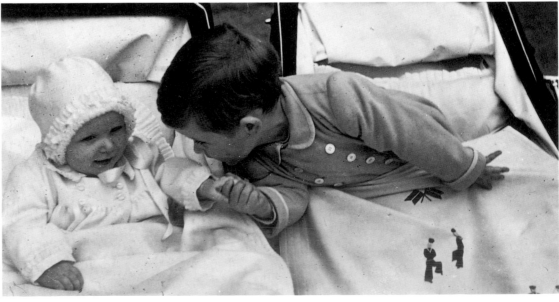

RIGHT: *The baby Princess Anne is ministered to by a solicitous Prince Charles.*

Prince derives a large part of his income from this estate – and pays tax on it.

No-one can doubt that Prince Charles has worked to live up to the Prince of Wales' motto *Ich Dien* [I serve]. The royal family's public rôle is closely linked to their private lives, and in the eyes of newspaper editors they appear almost inseparable. Prince Charles' private life has been the subject of intense speculation since he was in his late teens. Dubbed 'the world's most eligible bachelor' by the press during the 1970s, the Prince gave his views on marriage in an interview when he was 20: 'You've got to remember, in my position, you are going to marry someone who perhaps one day is going to be Queen. You've got to choose very carefully. The one advantage about marrying someone from a royal family is that they know what happens'. His name was linked with several European princesses, as well as a string of well-born British beauties, while the Prince was in his twenties, but he showed no sign of marrying. He once said that 'about 30' was the right time to marry, and it is alleged that the Queen and Prince Philip were keen for their eldest son to settle down once he had passed this milestone.

The Prince of Wales' romance and marriage in 1981 to Lady Diana Spencer is probably the most

LEFT AND TOP RIGHT: *There is only two years' age difference between Prince Charles and Princess Anne: they therefore spent much of their childhood together.*

OPPOSITE, BELOW LEFT: *Prince Charles attended Kensington School before becoming a boarder at Cheam in the autumn of 1957.*

OPPOSITE, BELOW RIGHT: *Princess Alexandra, Prince Charles and Prince Michael of Kent visit Lerwick in the Shetland Islands in 1960.*

exhaustively documented royal story in the world. Twelve years older than his 20-year-old bride, the Prince said that they shared a love of music and dancing and a similar sense of humour. 'I'm positively delighted and frankly amazed that Diana's prepared to take me on', he said, but one wonders whether his young bride really comprehended how enormously her life was about to change. Diana had been hounded by the British press during her courtship, but even this could not have prepared her for the insatiable public interest in her. In a sense the Princess of Wales has grown up in public, metamorphosing from blushing 19-year-old to the sophisticated and professional royal that she is today. Her every move has been monitored obsessively by the press, imposing an intolerable pressure on the Princess herself, as well as on her marriage. Eleven years after the world's most famous wedding, the principal players drifted apart and, at the end of 1992, their separation was announced.

The Prince spends long hours in solitary leisure pursuits like painting or shooting; the Princess devotes herself to the children, Princes William and Harry. Gone are the days when a starry-eyed Diana spent hours watching Charles playing polo. In the early days of their marriage they carried out public engagements together, with the Prince instructing his wife in the arts of the royal walkabout and regal wave. They now appear together on ceremonial state occasions and at family gatherings, but no longer seem to enjoy each other's company as much as they did.

Both the Prince and Princess of Wales work extremely hard. They have both demonstrated a very real interest in the lives of their future subjects and a commitment to the traditional duties of the royal family. It would be a pity if their potential was wasted, sacrificed to the hypocritical demands of tabloid editors and the more outdated traditions of the British constitution.

OPPOSITE, LEFT: *The Prince rehearses for a Cambridge University revue, 1969.*

BOTTOM, FAR LEFT: *At the Braemar Games.*

BOTTOM, LEFT: *The Prince is pictured fishing in 1969.*

ABOVE, TOP: *Go-karting with Prince Edward, 1969.*

ABOVE: *In 1969 Prince Charles received the Freedom of Cardiff on behalf of the Royal Regiment of Wales.*

RIGHT: *An informal portrait taken at Balmoral to celebrate Prince Charles' eighteenth birthday in 1966.*

RIGHT AND BELOW: *On 1 July 1969 Prince Charles was invested at Caernarvon Castle as Prince of Wales. His 'contemporary' coronet had been especially designed for the Prince, and Charles himself gained much public approval by making a speech in Welsh.*

ABOVE AND FACING PAGE: *The Colonel in Chief of the Parachute Regiment, and a qualified pilot in the Fleet Air Arm, the Prince has never been afraid to test himself to the limit.*

THESE PAGES: *In the 1970s Prince Charles was considered one of the world's most eligible bachelors, and was rarely seen without an attractive escort. Each new girlfriend drove the press into a fever of excitement and speculation as to a possible engagement.*

LEFT: *With Lady Jane Wellesley, the daughter of the Duke of Wellington, in 1972.*

BELOW, LEFT AND RIGHT: *The Prince's friendship with Davina Sheffield, seen here in 1976, provoked much conjecture.*

ABOVE, LEFT AND RIGHT: *Lady Sarah Spencer was a constant companion of Prince Charles in the late 1970s. In 1977 she introduced her younger sister Diana to the Prince of Wales, an introduction which was to have lasting repercussions.*

RIGHT: *Prince Charles and Sabrina Guinness.*

OPPOSITE PAGE AND ABOVE:
*Royal tours often involve the
wearing of a variety of exotic
headgear. In Canada Prince
Charles smokes a peace pipe
(above), and later wears a head-
dress and war-paint entirely
suited to the occasion
(opposite).*

LEFT: *Now sporting a stetson,
the Prince shares a private
joke with his brother,
Prince Andrew.*

203

THESE PAGES: *An appreciative guest, Prince Charles has found a warm welcome all over the world. He is always ready to enter into the spirit of the occasion, as these photographs show.*

TOP LEFT: *In the middle of a dance line in Fiji.*

LEFT: *Attired in national dress in Ghana.*

RIGHT: *Appropriately garbed and garlanded in India.*

206

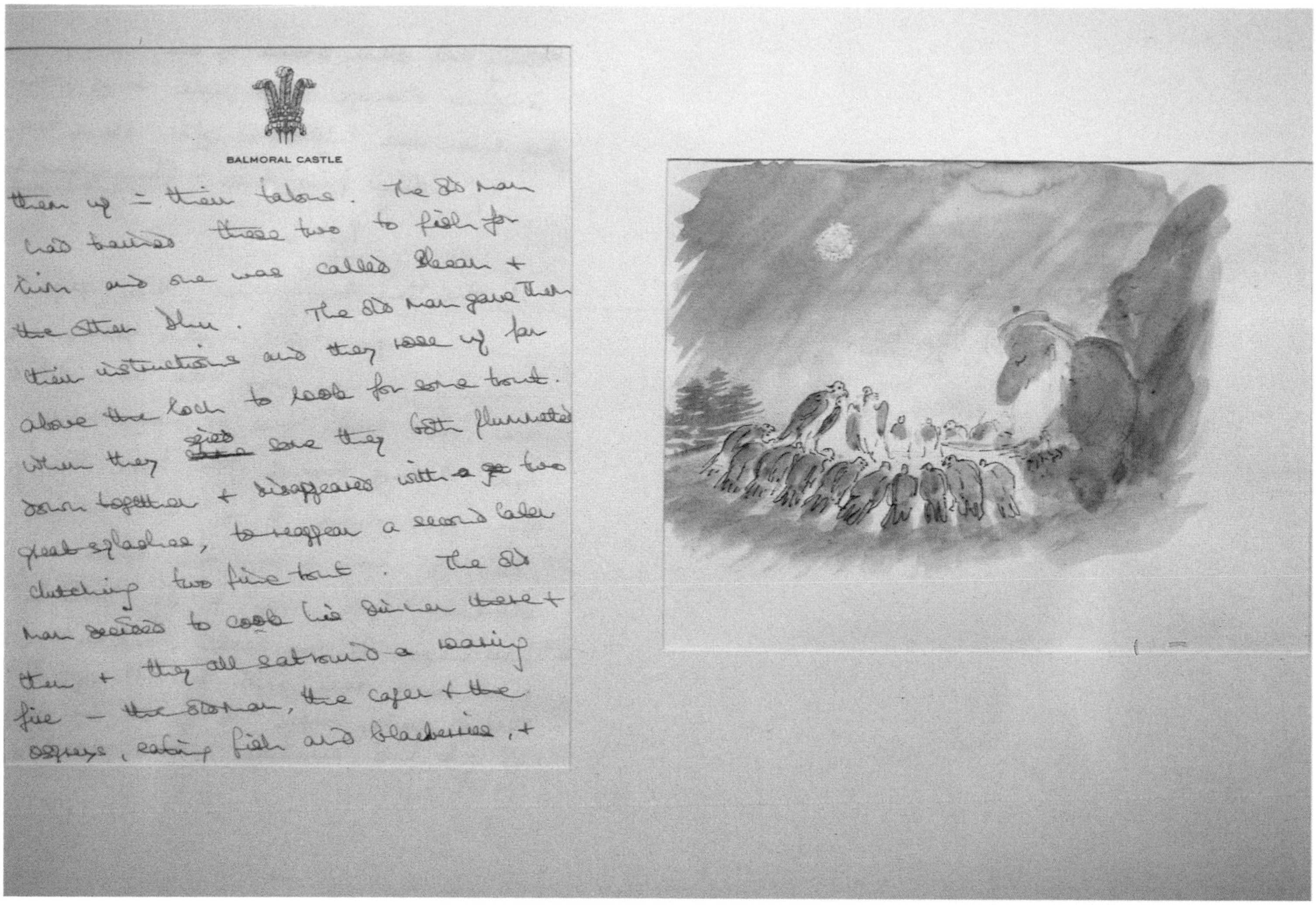

BALMORAL CASTLE

them up in their talons. The old man
had trained these two to fish for
him and one was called [illegible] +
the other Blue. The old man gave them
their instructions and they rose up far
above the loch to look for some trout.
When they ~~[illegible]~~ spied some they both plummeted
down together + disappeared with two
great splashes, to reappear a second later
clutching two fine trout. The old
man decided to cook his dinner there +
then + they all sat round a roaring
fire – the old man, the [illegible] + the
ospreys, eating fish and blackberries, +

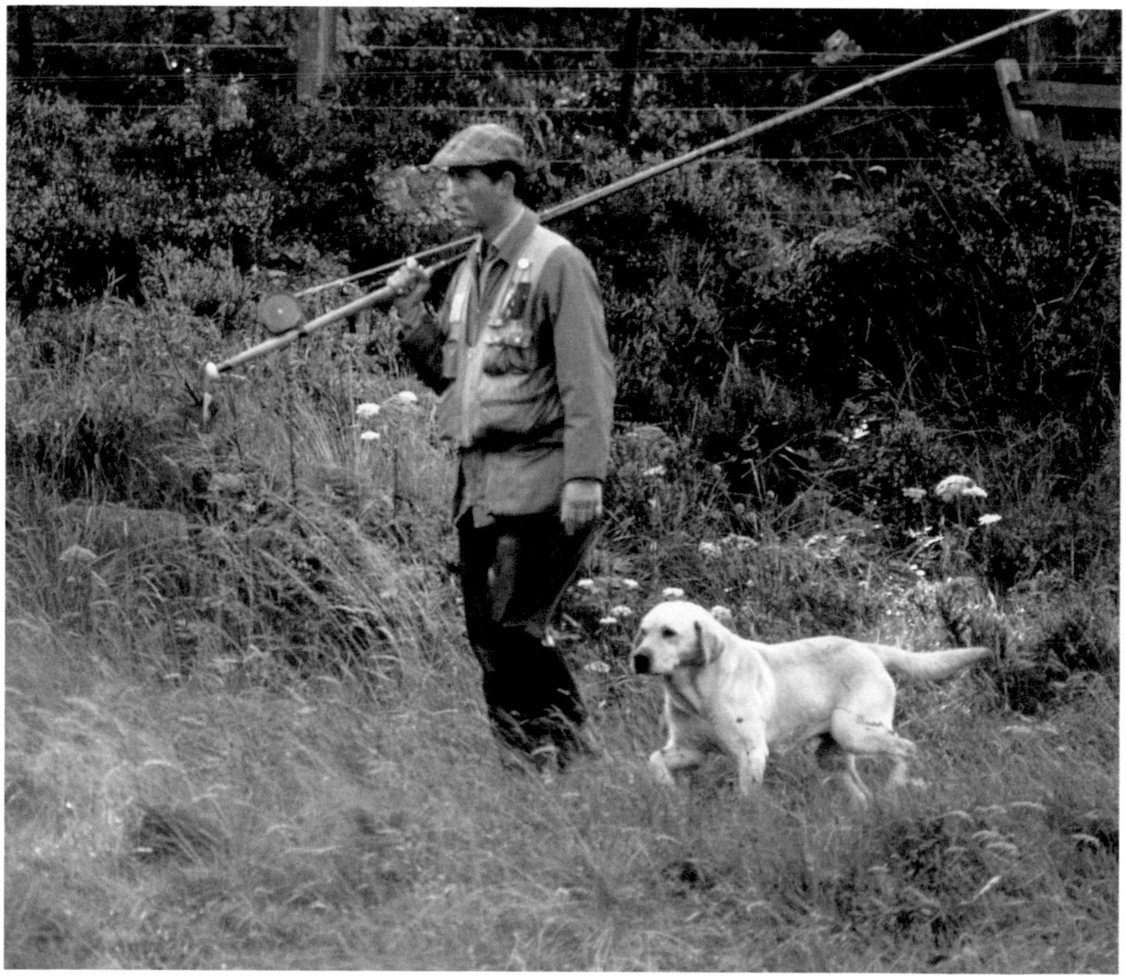

ABOVE: *Prince Charles wrote* The Old Man of Lochnagar *for his five-year-old brother Edward. It has since become a bestseller.*

LEFT AND RIGHT: *The Prince shares the royal family's love of sporting and country pursuits. Left: An uncharacteristically bearded Prince Charles on horseback at Badminton. Right: Like the Queen Mother, Prince Charles enjoys the peaceful diversion offered by freshwater fishing.*

THIS PAGE: *Prince Charles has turned his hand to many – often dangerous – sports over the years, including skiing, steeplechasing, polo, windsurfing, and shooting.*

OPPOSITE PAGE: *Trekking in the Himalayas.*

OPPOSITE PAGE: *Lord Mountbatten – 'Uncle Dickie' to Prince Philip, and Prince Charles' beloved great-uncle – was assassinated by IRA bombers in August 1979 while he was on a fishing trip in County Sligo in Ireland. His death was a devastating blow to the royal family.*

TOP LEFT: *Lord Mountbatten accompanies Prince Charles to Nepal, 1975.*

BOTTOM LEFT: *Prince Charles reads the lesson at Lord Mountbatten's funeral.*

RIGHT: *Resplendent in uniform. Prince Charles is the Colonel-in-Chief of six regiments, including the Welsh Guards and the Parachute Regiment. Here he wears the uniform of the Welsh Guards, with the wings of the Parachute Regiment on his sash.*

RIGHT: *Princess Diana has now been the subject of relentless public scrutiny for over a decade. At times the pressure must seem almost unbearable.*

THIS PAGE: *The 19-year-old Lady Diana Spencer was a shy kindergarten teacher until her engagement to Prince Charles on 24 February 1981 catapulted her into the limelight. The nation was enchanted by her, and her famous hairstyle became the most copied look in the land.*

ABOVE: *Prince Charles rides next to a rather overwhelmed Lady Diana at her first Royal Ascot.*

LEFT: *Diana's off-the-shoulder evening gown, worn for her first public engagement at Goldsmith's Hall, London, caused a sensation.*

LEFT: *A delighted Queen poses with the newly-engaged couple at Buckingham Palace, 1981.*

OVERLEAF: *A radiant bride. Earl Spencer prepares to lead his youngest daughter to the altar of St Paul's Cathedral. Lady Diana's spectacular train measured 25 feet.*

TOP AND LEFT: *Obviously enjoying each other's company, the royal couple fulfil a public engagement together (top) and take an enthusiastic turn on the dance floor (left).*

ABOVE AND RIGHT: *The royal honeymooners on the deck of the Britannia and (right) in Scotland.*

LEFT: *Prince William, the Prince and Princess of Wales' firstborn son, was born on 21 June 1982. Here the new addition to the Wales family leaves St Mary's Hospital, Paddington, with his parents.*

RIGHT: *Princess Diana holds Prince William at his christening.*

BELOW LEFT: *Both parents were obviously delighted with their baby son.*

BELOW RIGHT: *In a break with tradition, Prince William accompanied his parents on a tour of Australia and New Zealand when still under a year old.*

ABOVE: *Prince Charles meets local residents in Charleston, South Carolina, 1990.*

BELOW: *In the build-up to the Gulf War, Prince Charles visited a military camp in Saudi Arabia and boosted the morale of US Marines, 1990.*

ABOVE AND OPPOSITE, BELOW RIGHT: *In 1985 the Prince and Princess of Wales visited the United States, and were welcomed to the White House by President and Mrs Reagan.*

OPPOSITE, TOP RIGHT: *Prince Charles addresses the American Institute of Architects in 1990. He is famed for his firmly-held and often outspoken views on modern architecture.*

THE AMERICAN INSTITUTE OF ARCHITECTS

LEFT: *Princess Diana meets the actor Kenneth Branagh in Budapest, 1990.*

BELOW, FAR LEFT: *The Prince and Princess of Wales represent the Queen at Emperor Akihito of Japan's enthronement in 1990. The couple are accomplished ambassadors for Britain.*

BELOW LEFT: *Visiting Prague, in 1991.*

ABOVE AND RIGHT: *Princess Diana enjoys many aspects of popular culture. Here she is seen talking to David Bowie at the Live Aid concert in 1985 (above); and with Prince Charles at the Cannes Film Festival (right).*

227

LEFT, RIGHT, AND BELOW
LEFT: *The royal couple enjoy a warm relationship with King Juan Carlos and Queen Sofia of Spain. The families have often shared holidays in Majorca (right and below left), during which they are able to relax and unwind.*

FAR LEFT: *Prince Charles on the beach in Sardinia, 1991.*

RIGHT: *Uninhibited laughter from the Prince and Princess of Wales at a revue in Cameroon, 1990.*

THESE PAGES: *Prince Charles and Princess Diana have increasingly developed separate rôles within the family 'firm'.*

LEFT AND BELOW: *Prince Charles is well known for his interest in ecology and his concern for the environment.*

LEFT: *The royal family do their utmost to be supportive in times of crisis. Here the Prince and Princess of Wales are pictured on a visit to the victims of flooding in Wales.*

LEFT: *Princess Diana visits the Royal Military College, Sandhurst in 1987, her outfit wittily echoing the young officers' uniforms.*

ABOVE: *Inspecting her regiment, the Princess of Wales' Own, in 1991. The Princess clearly enjoys occasions such as these.*

LEFT: *The Prince and Princess of Wales as guests of honour in a Maori war canoe. Princess Diana evidently appreciated the incongruity of the situation.*

LEFT: *Princess Diana rides in the Queen's carriage to the state opening of Parliament.*

BELOW LEFT: *The royal couple represent Britain in Paris, 1988.*

OPPOSITE PAGE: *Despite their high public profile, the royal couple still manage to lead a relatively ordinary private life, spending time with their children whenever possible.*

TOP RIGHT: *Prince William and Prince Harry wave from the deck of* Britannia *as they leave Toronto with their parents on a visit to Canada.*

RIGHT: *The Princess of Wales takes Prince William to Wetherby School for his first day, 1987.*

FAR RIGHT: *The press corps surround Princess Diana on the ski slopes. It was on a skiing holiday such as this that she heard of the death of her father, Earl Spencer.*

LEFT: *The royal family always makes a considerable effort to be with the Queen Mother on her birthday. Pictured with her on the occasion of her ninety-second birthday are the Prince and Princess of Wales, Prince Andrew and Prince Harry.*

RIGHT: *Prince William undertakes his first public engagement, fittingly in Wales, in 1991.*

ABOVE AND RIGHT: *Both the Prince and Princess of Wales are true professionals in carrying out their public duties.*

THIS PAGE: *An accomplished sportsman, polo is one of Prince Charles' passions. However, he recently suffered a serious break to his arm (below right).*

OPPOSITE PAGE: *A light-hearted moment during an official engagement.*

CHAPTER EIGHT
ROYALTY TODAY

The question of the relevance of the royal family to modern society is one that has been raised again and again. At the end of the twentieth century many argue that the House of Windsor is, at best, little more than an expensive tourist attraction, and at worst a lurid soap opera funded by the taxpayer. The monarchy, however, is a unique institution providing Britain with an apolitical head of state who represents a focus of allegiance. There is nothing remotely democratic about an hereditary monarchy, but in a sovereign parliamentary democracy such as Britain the whole system is dependent on popular consent for survival. As Prince Philip once said: 'The answer to this question of the monarchy is very simple – if people don't like it, they should change it . . . The monarchy exists not for its own benefit, but for that of the country'.

Few of her subjects would doubt the Queen's personal devotion to her job, and after 40 years on the throne she is the most respected member of her family. Her relations are another matter. When the Queen came to the throne in 1952, there were only three working members of the direct royal family to support her: the Queen Mother, Princess Margaret and the Duke of Edinburgh. Forty years later there were nine (the original three, plus her four children and two daughters-in-law). In addition, the Queen's cousins, the Dukes of Gloucester and Kent, Princess Alexandra and Prince Michael of Kent, also take their share of official duties. The nuclear family, as Anthony Jay wrote in *Elizabeth R*, has turned into something of a dynasty.

The public has a schizophrenic attitude to the modern royal family, on the one hand expecting them to earn their Civil List allowances by 'showing the flag', and behaving with the decorum one would expect of public figures; on the other, demanding to see them as 'ordinary' people, and pandering to the tabloid desire to treat them in the same way as less blue-blooded members of the jet set. It is not, therefore, particularly surprising when, subject to the constant pressure of powerfully intrusive camera lenses, those who were not born to the job occasionally show an all too human face. One only has to think of the allegations about the Duchess of York's behaviour on an aeroplane in early 1992 when she apparently threw packets of sugar over members of the press corps. Similarly, the Princess of Wales is widely rumoured to have suffered from bulimia, and even to have attempted suicide during her early years in the public eye.

The Queen's children may envy their cousins, Lady Sarah Armstrong-Jones and Viscount Linley, who have for the most part been allowed to get on with their lives relatively free from media intervention. Princess Margaret has remarked that her children are not royal, they merely have the Queen for an aunt. Any perceived transgression, however, is instantly snatched on with glee by the media. Marina Ogilvy, the daughter of Princess Alexandra, fell out with her parents in a public display of temper when she became pregnant before she was married. The world waited to see whether she would produce the first (acknowledged) royal bastard for nearly 200 years, but she married her commoner lover before the birth of their daughter.

The fascination of the world's press with the House of Windsor is unending. As individuals the family are not extraordinary, but the mystique of royalty evidently still is. A touch from the Queen no longer cures scrofula, 'the King's evil', but a photogenic smile from her or one of her relatives sells hundreds of thousands of magazines and newspapers.

The royal family exist today in a glare of publicity that is bound to affect their lives. The Queen's children and grandchildren have grown up with the twin

RIGHT: *Queen Elizabeth II (foreground), surrounded by members of her family.*

pressures of being set apart from ordinary people by an accident of birth, and being the focus of unceasing public interest in their every move. The monarchy itself has been slow to adjust to the second of these pressures, preferring instead to delude itself that the world is still as deferential as it was 50 or 60 years ago. It seems unlikely that the ancient institution of the Crown will be toppled by the indiscretions of younger members of the family out of direct line to the throne, but there is no doubt that such antics lessen the dignity and respect accorded to the monarchy.

The royal family have worked long and hard to justify their Civil List allowances. The work of Princess Anne, for example, as President of Save the Children has been invaluable to that organization; similarly, the Princess of Wales' concern for AIDS victims has helped to enlighten people about the disease. Many members of the royal family have the ability to raise morale and encourage people simply by their presence. Ceremonial occasions, such as the annual opening of Parliament by the Queen, or her presence at the head of her army during the Trooping of the Colour, serve to emphasize the unique tradition behind Britain's system of government. The British monarchy is an ancient institution that could be abolished constitutionally if the country wished to. However, the very fact that it provides the nation with a degree of stability and is generally a force for good in a changing world should make potential republicans think twice before attempting to do so.

240

LEFT AND BELOW: *Princess Margaret married society photographer Anthony Armstrong-Jones (Lord Snowdon), at Westminster Abbey on 6 May 1960.*

RIGHT: *The son of the Earl and Countess of Snowdon, David, Viscount Linley, was born in 1961; their daughter, Lady Sarah Armstrong-Jones followed in 1964.*

ABOVE: *Princess Margaret has a relaxed yet supportive relationship with her children, both of whom have inherited their parents' interest in the arts. Lady Sarah Armstrong-Jones is a respected artist, while Viscount Linley has his own furniture workshop.*

THIS PAGE: *Princess Margaret's children (top left, in the 1960s) have suffered far less media pressure than the Queen's children. However, they are close to their cousins and spent a lot of time together in childhood.*

ABOVE: *Prince Edward and Lady Sarah Armstrong-Jones accompany their grandmother, the Queen Mother, to the Royal College of Music in 1969.*

LEFT: *The royal family leave London by train for Sandringham, 1969; from left: Prince Andrew, Prince Edward, Lady Sarah Armstrong-Jones, Viscount Linley and, behind, Prince Charles and the Queen.*

ABOVE AND LEFT: *There had been rumours of marital difficulties between Princess Margaret and Lord Snowdon since the late 1960s. In 1976 their decision to separate was finally made public and was followed by divorce in 1978.*

TOP LEFT: *Princess Margaret holidaying in Mustique.*

OPPOSITE PAGE: *An official portrait of the Queen's younger sister.*

BELOW: *Prince Charles and Princess Margaret attend the opening of the David Linley Workshop in 1987.*

ABOVE LEFT: *Prince Richard of Gloucester married Birgitte Deurs, a Danish citizen, in 1972.*

LEFT: *The marriage of Princess Alexandra of Kent to Angus Ogilvy, 1963.*

ABOVE: *The royal family wave from the deck of the* Britannia *on the occasion of Prince Charles' first visit to Wales in 1960.*

RIGHT: *Prince Charles and Princess Anne with the junior royals in 1969. From left: James Ogilvy, Lady Sarah Armstrong-Jones, the Earl of St Andrews, Lady Helen Windsor, Viscount Linley, Prince Andew, Marina Ogilvy, Prince Edward.*

247

LEFT: *Princess Anne, her mother and aunt in 1951, aged one year. She enjoyed a relatively carefree childhood before being sent to school at Benenden in Kent.*

BELOW: *Sharing a joke with Prince Charles in 1952.*

RIGHT: *Princess Anne has inherited her mother's love of horses. They are seen here in 1955 with Greensleeves.*

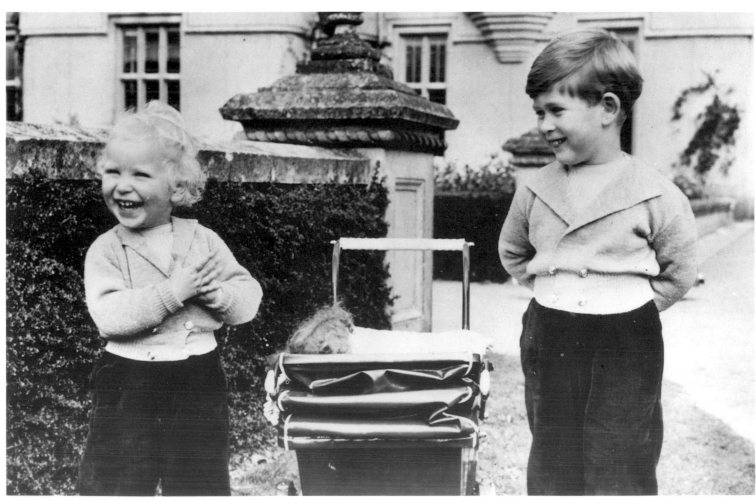

ABOVE, LEFT AND RIGHT:
*Riding has consistently
dominated Princess Anne's life.
It has given her the chance to
compete on equal terms at the
highest level: 'If I am good at it,
I'm good at it – and not because
I'm Princess Anne'. Competing
in her first steeplechase at
Windsor in 1968 (above left).
Riding Doublet at the Bridge
House Trials in 1969 (above
right).*

RIGHT: *Dressed in riding
outfits, the Queen and Princess
Anne prepare to take a boat out
at Frogmore, 1959.*

OPPOSITE PAGE: *A glamorous
portrait of Princess Anne, taken
to mark her twenty-first
birthday in 1971.*

THESE PAGES: *Their mutual love of horses brought Princess Anne and Captain Mark Phillips, a career soldier, together (left). Indeed, in 1971 Princess Anne came fifth in the Badminton Horse Trials; the winner was her future husband. Their engagement in May 1973 (right) was followed by a November wedding at Westminster Abbey (above).*

254

LEFT: *The wedding of Princess Anne and Captain Mark Phillips was followed in 1977 by the birth of their son, Peter Phillips. He was the first royal child for centuries to be born a commoner.*

BELOW, FAR LEFT: *The christening of Peter Phillips, December 1977.*

BELOW, LEFT AND RIGHT: *In 1976 both Princess Anne and her husband were selected to represent Britain as members of the equestrian team at the Olympic Games held at Montreal in Canada. Both competitors acquitted themselves with skill.*

LEFT: *Princess Anne has a particularly strong bond with her father; they are very similar in character and have great respect for each other.*

FAR LEFT, LEFT, AND RIGHT: *Zara Phillips was born in May 1981; even after their parents' separation and divorce Peter and Zara remain close to both their parents and share their interests.*

257

THESE PAGES: *Princess Anne is the hardest-working member of the royal family and carries out hundreds of official engagements each year*

OPPOSITE PAGE: *The Princess Royal in the robes of the Chancellor of London University.*

ABOVE: *Relaxing with her younger brother, Prince Andrew.*

LEFT AND BELOW: *A tireless ambassador for Save the Children, Princess Anne frequently travels the world in its cause.*

THESE PAGES: *Both the Princess Royal and Captain Mark Phillips have done their utmost to shield their children from public scrutiny. However, Peter and Zara Phillips have a warm relationship with their royal relations.*

OPPOSITE: *A relaxed Princess Anne.*

LEFT: *Edward, the present Duke of Kent, inherited his title in 1942, after the tragic death of his father. In 1961 he married Katharine Worsley. Their three children are George, Earl of St Andrews, Lady Helen Taylor and Lord Nicholas Windsor.*

RIGHT: *The Duchess of Kent, pictured with her elegant daughter, Lady Helen, whose marriage in 1992 put an end to a frenzy of press speculation.*

TOP, FAR LEFT AND LEFT: *The engagement of the Duke of Kent's younger brother, Prince Michael of Kent, to Baroness Marie-Christine von Reibnitz in 1978 (top, far left) caused enormous controversy. In order to marry her, a Catholic whose first marriage had been annulled, Prince Michael had to renounce his claim to the throne, while she had to agree that their children would be brought up as Anglicans.*

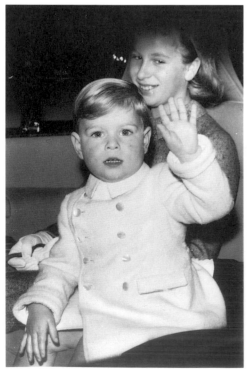

THESE PAGES: *Prince Andrew was born in February 1960, and the Queen's family was completed by the birth in March 1964 of Prince Edward. There is a 10-year gap between Princess Anne and Prince Andrew. The Queen and Duke of Edinburgh were far more relaxed with their 'second' family, and their youngest sons responded accordingly.*

265

THIS PAGE: *Although Prince Andrew was for the most part educated at Gordonstoun in Scotland, he spent some time as a pupil at Lakefield College in Canada. His gregarious nature and good looks made him very popular, particularly with the opposite sex.*

OPPOSITE PAGE: *In 1976 Princess Anne competed in the Olympic Games in Montreal; despite the occasionally unsporting weather, her family turned out to support her.*

ABOVE LEFT: *Nancy Reagan watches polo at Windsor in 1981, escorted by the Prince.*

ABOVE RIGHT: *Prince Andrew sporting a short-lived beard.*

BELOW AND RIGHT: *A career naval officer, Prince Andrew saw action in the Falklands Campaign in 1982; right HMS* Invincible's *return from the Falklands.*

RIGHT: *Prince Andrew was mobbed in Canada, 1985.*

THIS PAGE: *The Duke of York is a fearless helicopter pilot (above right). After his engagement to Sarah Ferguson (above left and below right) in 1986, his fiancée resolved to share this interest, taking flying lessons and qualifying as a pilot herself.*

THESE PAGES: *On 23 July 1986, amid a heady atmosphere of public hysteria and ancient pomp and pageantry, Prince Andrew married Sarah Ferguson at Westminster Abbey. Yet only six years later the newly-created Duke and Duchess of York were to announce their separation.*

THESE PAGES: *Both exuberant and high-spirited characters, the Duke and Duchess of York seemed a perfect match for each other. Both enjoyed the challenge of outdoor pursuits, such as flying, exploring and skiing. They also shared a boisterous sense of humour.*

ABOVE AND RIGHT: *The daughters of the Duke and Duchess of York, Princess Beatrice (above) and Princess Eugenie (right) were born in 1988 and 1990 respectively. Their unusual names reflect the couple's affinity with the Victorian era.*

THIS PAGE: *The formal separation of the Duke and Duchess of York was announced in 1992. Although the young princesses are living with their mother, they frequently spend time in the company of their father.*

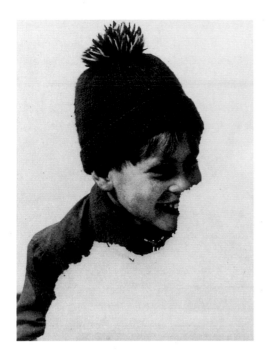

ABOVE: The young Prince Edward enjoying a snowball fight.

TOP LEFT: *Prince Edward with his father in Canada, 1976.*

FAR LEFT: *After leaving Gordonstoun, Prince Edward was briefly employed as a school teacher in New Zealand.*

CENTRE LEFT: *Prince Edward at RAF Benson in 1989; unlike his brothers he has not wished to pursue a career in the armed forces.*

BELOW LEFT: *Windsurfing during Cowes Week.*

ABOVE: *An informal portrait of the Prince with his pet labrador.*

RIGHT: *The Queen and Duke of Edinburgh pay a visit to their youngest son at Jesus College, Cambridge, where he was studying in 1984.*

THESE PAGES: *In many ways Prince Edward has been able to lead a less regimented life than his elder brothers. His unconventional decision to work in the theatrical world was a brave step to take. However, in common with their love of riding and sailing, like the rest of the family he is also dedicated to his royal duties and is a keen promoter of the Duke of Edinburgh's Award Scheme.*

ABOVE: *Lady Sarah Armstrong-Jones was born in the same year as her cousin, Prince Edward.*

ABOVE RIGHT: *Lady Sarah with her brother, Viscount Linley and the Queen Mother.*

OPPOSITE PAGE, TOP LEFT: *Lady Sarah has inherited her parents' artistic flair, and is a talented painter in her own right.*

OPPOSITE PAGE, TOP RIGHT: *Prince Edward with his sister, the Princess Royal.*

RIGHT: *The Queen, flanked by her youngest sons, Prince Andrew and Prince Edward.*

THESE PAGES: *There were some happy moments in 1992, such as the wedding of Lady Helen Windsor (opposite page, top left), and Princess Anne's marriage to Commander Timothy Laurence. However, the year also witnessed the breakdown of the marriages of the Prince of Wales and the Duke of York, and a fire seriously damaged Windsor Castle. The royal family tried to put a brave face things.*

FAR RIGHT: *Watching the Remembrance Day ceremony in London.*

PREVIOUS PAGES: *Four generations of the royal family wave to the crowds from the famous balcony at Buckingham Palace.*

ABOVE: *The children of Queen Elizabeth II and the Duke of Edinburgh to the fore: the destiny of the royal family and, indeed, of the British monarchy, lies in their hands.*

INDEX

Figures in *italics* refer to illustrations

abdication of Edward VIII
(1936) 72-73, *84*, 98,
102-03, 124, 144
Aberfan mining disaster
(1966) 150
Akihito, Emperor of Japan
enthronement (1990)
226
Albert, Prince, consort to
Queen Victoria 6, *8*,
10, *12*, 20
Albert Victor, Prince 20, 22,
26, 29, 30, 42, 44, *44*,
45, 47
Alexandra, Queen 20,
22-27, 29, 33, 35, 37, *40*
Alexandra, Princess of Kent
162, *195*, 238, *246*
Alexis, Tsarevich of Russia
14, *49*
Alfonso XIII, King of Spain
33
Alice, Princess, Duchess of
Gloucester 65, *85*, 132,
134, 162
Alice, Princess of Greece *151*
Andrew, Prince 2, *138*, *140*,
146, 148, 149, *173*, *174*,
176, 203, *218*, 234, 243,
247, *259*, 264-66,
268-76, *286-87*
Anne, Princess Royal *121*,
138, 148-49, *158*, 172,
173, 176, *177*, 193-95,
240, *247-59*, 267, *281*,
283, *286-87*
Armstrong-Jones, Anthony,
Earl of Snowdon *170*,
171, 240-41, *244*
Armstrong-Jones, Lady
Sarah *138*, *140*, 238,
241-43, *247*, *280*, *281*
Army 20, 22, 26, 70, 99, 144,
150, *197*, 198, *199*, 211,
231
Ascot races 61, *81*, 119, *185*,
215
Asquith, Herbert 22, 45
Attlee, Clement *164*
Australia
Prince Charles' stay in
190
royal tours 44, 70, 72, *79*,
80, 101, *128*, 223

Bagehot, Walter 6
Bahamas
Edward VIII Governor of
88, 89
opening of Parliament by
Elizabeth II (1973) *178*
Baldwin, Stanley 72, *81*
Beatrice, Princess, daughter
of Prince Andrew 2,
274, 275
Beatrice, Princess, daughter
of Queen Victoria *16*
Bowie, David 227
Braemar Games *196*
Branagh, Kenneth *226*
Britannia, royal yacht *178*,
220, *233*, *246*
HMS *Bronington* 190
Brown, John *14*

Cambridge University 20,
98, 190, *196*, 277
Canada
Prince Andrew pupil *266*
royal tours and visits 70,
76, *77*, *114*, 124, *137*,
157, *167*, 203, 268 see

also Olympic Games
Chamberlain, Neville *115*
Channon, Chips 72, 126
Charles, Prince *3*, *138*, *142*,
176, 190, *195-97*, 211,
228, 229, 235, 237, 243,
245-48, *286-87*
childhood 104, *121*, *158*,
172, *173*, 190, *192-96*
education 148, 190, *194*
environment 190, *230*
family *143*, 194, 222, 223,
233, *234*
investiture as Prince of
Wales (1969) *190*, *198*
leisure *196*, *206-09*
marriage to Lady Diana
Spencer (1981) 193-94,
214-15, *218-21*,
separation 194, 282
naval career 190
Old Man of Lochnagar, The,
book by 207
polo-playing *188*, *191*, 194,
236
private life in 1970s 149,
193, *200-01*
tours and visits *202-05*,
223-27, 231, 232
China, visit by Elizabeth
II and Prince Philip 184
Christmas message
first wireless broadcast by
George V (1934) *68*
first television by
Elizabeth II (1957) *167*
Churchill, Winston 104, *115*,
121, 146, *161*
Civil List allowances 238,
240
Clifton, Nellie 20
Commonwealth and
Elizabeth II 146-47, *165*,
180
coronations
1838 Victoria *9*, *11*
1901 Edward VII 32, *33*,
44
1911 George V *2*, *52*
1937 George VI *103*, *110*,
111, *132*
1953 Elizabeth II *4*, 144,
146, *160-64*
deaths and funerals
1892 Prince Albert Victor
22, *42*, 44
1901 Victoria 6, *18*, *19*
1910 Edward VII *40*, *41*
1936 George V *45*, *68*, *69*
1952 George VI *91*, 104,
122-23
1972 Edward VIII 73, *96*,
97
1979 Lord Mountbatten
210, *211*
Delhi Durbar (1911) *52*
Deurs, Birgitte, Duchess of
Gloucester 246
Diamond Jubilee of Queen
Victoria (1897) *13*, 22
Diana, Princess of Wales 2,
3, 193-94, *212-23*,
225-35, 238, 240

Edward VII, King *2*, *3*, 6,
18, 20, *21*, 22, *22*, *23*,
27-30, *37-39*, 45, *74*
coronation (1901) 32,
33, 44
death and funeral (1910)
40, *41*
education 20
Entente Cordiale 22, *36*
family 20, 22, 25, 26, *30*,
34, *35*
marriage to Princess
Alexandra of Denmark
(1863) 20, *23-25*
tour of India (1875) 22

Edward, Duke of Windsor
2, *8*, 35, *48*, *49*, *56*, 57,
65, 70, 72, 73, 78, *80*,
81, *85*, 90-95, 102, *102*,
103, 144
abdication 72-73, *84*, 98,
102-03, 124, 144
affairs 72
autobiography, *A King's
Story* 93
death 73, *96*, 97
education 70
exile in France 73, *92*, *93*
Governor of the Bahamas
88, 89
investiture as Prince of
Wales (1911) 70, *74*
meeting and marriage to
Mrs Wallis Simpson
72-73, *81-85*, 102
title after abdicating 73
tours 70, 72, 76, *77*, *79*, *80*
World War I 70, *75*
World War II *87*
Edward, Prince, son of
Elizabeth II *138*, 148,
149, *174*, *176*, *197*, *207*,
243, *247*, *264*, *265*,
276-81, *286-87*
Edward, Prince, Duke of
Kent *162*, 238, *262*, *263*
Elizabeth II, Queen *1-3*, 6,
72, 95, 144, *145*, 146-50,
167, *178-79*, *182-89*, *214*,
238, 240, 243, 249, 250,
277
childhood 65, 101, *108*,
109, 124, *128*, 130, *132*,
144, *146*, *147*
coronation (1953) 144, 146,
160-64
education 144
family *143*, 148, *158*, *159*,
172-74, 176, 193, *239*,
248, *281*
marriage to Philip
Mountbatten (1947)
104, *121*, 144, *152-56*
Silver Jubilee (1977) *177*
Silver Wedding (1972) *176*
taxation question 148
tours *168*, *175*, *181*, *184*
World War II *135*, 149
youth *101*, *118-20*, *133*,
148-50, 157
Elizabeth, Queen Mother *2*,
3, *56*, 102, *104*, *105*, *113*,
125-43, 149, *162*, *234*,
238, 243
80th birthday 124, *138*
family 101, *101*, 108, *109*,
119, *120*, 124, *128*, 130,
146, 149, 157
marriage to George VI
(1923) 98, 101, *106-07*,
124, *128*
resumption of official
duties (1953) 124, *134*
tours and state visits 101,
103, 104, *114*, 124, *128*,
132, *133*, 137
World War II 103-04, *116*,
118, 124, *135*, *141*
Eugenie, Princess,
daughter of Prince
Andrew *274*, 275
Eugenie, Queen of Spain *33*

Falklands Campaign, Prince
Andrew's service in
149, *268*
Ferguson, Sarah, Duchess
of York 238, *269-73*
Fiji, visit by Prince Charles
204
Fleet Air Arm
Prince Charles' service
with 190, *198*, *199*
France 22, *36*, 103, *114*,

151, 232
Edward VIII in 70, 73, *75*,
84, *85*, *87*, *92*
French, General John 70, *75*
funerals *see* deaths
Furness, Lady Thelma 72

garden parties,
Buckingham Palace *61*,
65, 147
George V, King *2*, *3*, *19*, *26*,
29, 30, 33, 34, 42, 43,
45, *46*, *49*, 53, *57-61*,
70, 72, 101, *106*, 144
accession 50, *51*
bronchial illness and
recovery 62-63
Christmas message by
wireless (1934) 68
coronation (1911) *2*, *52*
death and funeral (1936)
42, 45, *68*, *69*, 72, 101
Delhi Durbar (1911) *52*
education 42
family 35, 44, *48*, *49*, *56*,
70
marriage to Princess May
of Teck (1893) 42, 44,
46, 47, *47*
naval activities 42, *45*
Silver Jubilee (1935) *45*,
66, *67*
tours 34, 44
World War I *54*, *55*
George VI, King *3*, *49*, *56*,
72, 73, 98, *100-05*, 101,
113, *129*, *130*
abdication, effect on 102,
124
coronation (1937) *103*,
110-11, *132*
death and funeral (1952)
91, 104, *122-23*, 124,
144, *160*
deterioration of health
104, *119*, 124
education 98
family 101, *101*, 104, *108*,
109, *112*, *119-21*, 144,
146, 149, 157
marriage to Lady
Elizabeth Bowes-Lyon
(1923) 98, 101, *106-07*,
124
Navy 98
tours and state visits 101,
103, 104, *114*
World War I 98
World War II 98, 103-04,
112, *116-18*
George, Prince, Duke of
Kent *56*, *80*, 102, *117*, 132
George, Earl of St Andrews
247, 262
Germany 37, 45, 53, 103
Nazi interest in Edward
VIII 73, 86, 88
royal family *16*, 22, *33*, 37,
53
Ghana, visit by Prince
Charles 204
Gordonstoun School,
Scotland 148, *151*, 190
Guinness, Sabrina 201
Gulf War
London parade *188*
visit by Charles to camp
in Saudi Arabia 224

Hardie, Keir 70
Harry, Prince, son of
Prince Charles 194, *233*,
234
Henry, Prince, Duke of
Gloucester *49*, *56*, 65,
85, 132, *134*, 162
horse-racing interests 20,
22, 39, 78, 124, *136*,
182, *183*, *185*, *see also*

Ascot races

India
Delhi Durbar (1911) *52*
royal tours 22, 44, 70, *168*,
205
investiture of the Prince of
Wales
1911 Prince Edward 70,
74;
1969 Prince Charles *190*,
198
HMS *Invincible* 268
Ireland *17*, 20, *112*

Jay, Anthony 238
John Paul II, Pope *180*
Juan Carlos, King of Spain
228

King's Story, A,
autobiography of
Edward VIII 93
Kuwait, Emir of *181*

Lascelles, Viscount 57
Lawrence, Commander
Timothy 169, *283*
Leopold, Prince *15*
Linley, Viscount David *138*,
140, 238, *241-43*, *245*,
247, *280*
Live Aid concert (1985) *227*
Lloyd George, David 70
Logue, Lionel 101
London University *137*, *258*
Louise, Princess Royal *26*,
30, 45, *46*

MacDonald, Ramsay 45
Margaret, Princess *3*, *65*,
101, *101*, 109, *118-20*,
124, 130, *132-36*, *143*,
144, *146*, 148, *148-50*,
157, *162*, *169-71*, 238,
240, *242*, *244-45*, *248*
Marina, Princess, Duchess
of Kent *132*, *162*
marriages
1840 Victoria to Prince
Albert *8*
1863 Edward VII to
Princess Alexandra of
Denmark 20, *23-25*
1893 George V to Princess
May of Teck 42, 44, *46*,
47
1922 Princess Mary to
Viscount Lascelles 57
1923 George VI to Lady
Elizabeth Bowes-Lyon
98, 101, *106*, *107*
1935 Henry, Duke of
Gloucester to Lady
Alice Montague-
Douglas-Scott 65
1937 Edward VIII to
Wallis Simpson 72-73,
84-85
1953 Elizabeth II to Philip
Mountbatten 104, *121*,
144, *152-56*
1960 Princess Margaret to
Anthony Armstrong-
Jones 240, divorce 245
1963 Princess Alexandra
to Angus Ogilvy *246*
1972 Prince Richard of
Gloucester to Birgitte
Deurs *246*
1977 Princess Anne to
Captain Mark Phillips
254, divorce 257
1981 Prince Charles to
Lady Diana Spencer
193-94, *214-15*, *218-21*,
separation 194, 282
1986 Prince Andrew to
Sarah Ferguson *270-71*,

287